TURNING POINTS 2

ERIN ATHENE ◆ JESSICA JOBES

JASE SOUDER

Published by
Hybrid Global Publishing
333 E 14th Street
#3C
New York, NY 10003

Copyright © 2023 by Jase Souder

All rights reserved. No part of this book may be reproduced or transmitted in any form or by any means, electronic or mechanical, including photocopying, recording, or by any information storage and retrieval system, without the written permission of the Publisher, except where permitted by law.

Manufactured in the United States of America, or in the United Kingdom when distributed elsewhere.

Souder, Jase
Turning Points 2
     ISBN: 978-1-957013-70-1
     eBook: 978-1-957013-71-8

Cover design by: Joe Potter
Copyediting by: Claudia Volkman
Interior design by: Suba Murugan
Author photo by: Nikki Incandela

https://worldclassspeakeracademy.com/

CONTENTS

Introduction by Jase Souder vii

Turning Point—One or Many? by Kitti Andrews 9

Really?! That Is Not My Beautiful Life by Lauren Archibeque 15

The Problem Was Actually the Solution by Shiraz Baboo 21

A Place to Grow and Thrive by Cyndi Barnard 29

From Three Strikes to Home Run by Evan Barnard 35

The Undeniable Truth about Health by Jen Beck 41

Your Vision. Your Life. Your Way. by Kathleen Carlson 49

Wherever You Go, There You Are by Rachael Channing 55

The Pursuit of Craziness by Anna Y.C. Chen 61

Are You Lost at Sea? Thriving after Breast Cancer by Jenny C. Cohen 67

Breaking Out of Struggles and Leading Your Way! by Ramesh Dewangan ... 75

The Danger Zone by Sharon Galluzzo 81

CONTENTS

From Bankruptcy to Financial Peace of Mind—A Tale of Triumph
and Persistence by Michael Hession 87

Roller-Coaster Ride from Adversity to Triumph
by Karyn Marie Kokeny 93

The Making of a Mother by Janet Krebs 101

Living Life for YOU by Cat LaCohie 109

It Took Only Three Words by Deanna Litz 117

Why Your Lost Weight Keeps Finding You by Michele McHenry 125

What Is in Your Hand? From Tipping Point to Turning Point
by Tim Mitchell 131

From Farm Boy to Multimillionaire by Marlon Mueller 137

Lessons from a Struggling, Starving Stylist by Sara Murray 145

Let's Stop the Bullying in Healthcare! by Nanette Nuessle, MD 151

How Doing Something I Thought I Could Never Do Changed
My Life Forever by Dr. Mort Orman, MD 157

Take Back Your Life: From Goal-Oriented Overachiever to
Purpose-Driven High-Performer in Three Simple Steps
by Krys Pappius 163

Keep Your Light On by Roslyn Rasberry 171

From Broken to Whole by Mary Jo Rennert 177

Humanity Wins by Karen Rigamonti 185

Build a Business to Support Your Lifestyle by Lynne Roe 191

CONTENTS

Funding Your Dream by Lamont Stephens 199

Wouldn't It Be Funny by Patricia Stepler 205

All My World's a Stage by Jared Stull 211

Flipping the "Profit" Switch by Nichole Stull 219

From Being Suppressed to Being Expressed by Molly Anne Summers 225

Books Should Be Beautiful by Rachel Valliere 231

INTRODUCTION

Jase Souder

"Most people live their life like they're having a fitful dream.
They toss and turn and stay asleep, while those of us
who have had a nightmare wake ourselves up."

In your hands you hold a book about Turning Points.

What Is a Turning Point?

It's a time in life where someone made the pivot from suffering, despair, loneliness, depression, destitution, or poverty to a life of abundance, love, joy, happiness, hope, and health.

Turning Points are those moments when life changes.

Turning Points give us our mission.

Turning Points change our world and give us our capacity to change the world.

Why Are Turning Points Important?

First, let's look at the structure: There's a pretty clear path for a Turning Point. Usually it begins with life being OK and then something goes horribly wrong; there's a period of challenge when things get worse, bottom out, and then the Turning Point, followed by periods of growth and learning. The final phase of a Turning Point is using what's been learned to make a difference and change the world.

So, why is this important?

It's in the struggle that we get strong.

It's in the hopelessness that we find faith.

It's in the seeking a solution for our life that we find solutions the world needs.

It's in the Turning Point journey that you become a person who is equipped to make a difference.

If you're on the path toward your Turning Point right now, be encouraged.

This book is full of people who were in a downward spiral, too (maybe there's someone who went through exactly what you're going through), and they made it. They had their Turning Point, and now they are enjoying great lives. Let their stories speak to you and show you how you can make it, too.

If you've already had a Turning Point, maybe you're the next one to share.

Maybe you're feeling the pull to use your story and lessons to make an impact on the world. Let the courage, authenticity, and vulnerability of these authors inspire you to share your own Turning Point.

Kitti Andrews

Kitti Andrews, founder of Declutter the Brain!, is highly sought after by entrepreneurs who want to organize their space and streamline their thoughts so they can focus on profitable productivity. Her signature "ONE" system has helped hundreds of people to prioritize their time and mental energy to improve their bottom line.

www.declutterthebrain.com

TURNING POINT—ONE OR MANY?

Kitti Andrews

You are reading so many stories in this book about when someone had an exact "aha" moment that changed their life. I envy these people!

I'm often asked how I got into the business of helping people to organize their space and streamline their thoughts—aka mental and physical decluttering. I used to have difficulty with this question, but I think the opportunity to write this chapter is also a golden opportunity to pause and reflect on my life in search of an answer.

You see, I believe that for some of us, especially those blessed with ADHD (notice I said, "blessed"), there may not be one particular "lightning bolt from the sky" moment, but rather a series of small but life changing events that may go unnoticed at the time but, in retrospect, shape who we are now. Looking back at some of these moments can give us an idea of their compound effect on our life, whether that is good or bad.

For example, I vividly remember shopping for a winter coat with my mother when I was five years old and choosing a bright red parka with a white fur-trimmed hood. When my mother asked me why I chose that one, I proudly replied, "That's my favorite color"; the life moment there was not when she snarkily said, "That'll change," but when I mentally said, "No, it won't!" and wondered why she would question my judgment. For the record, red is still my favorite color. Lesson learned? I am often reminded of my lifelong inner resolve as well as my faith in my convictions and what I believe is right.

Fast-forward to my first year in a new high school in a new city. Not only was I the new kid, but also the new school nerd. However, that didn't stop me from approaching my crush and asking him out for coffee. I still remember the sting of his polite "I'm flattered, but no thank you" refusal. Shortly thereafter, a suavely dressed student asked me (ME! The nerd!) out for coffee. Lesson learned? When one door closes, another one opens.

This same coffee-seeking fellow, who seemed very wealthy and man-about-town, turned out to be a welfare recipient with negligible grades who was possibly earning the money for his expensive clothes through nefarious means. Lesson learned? Things are not always as they seem, but if you don't try, you don't know.

Growing up as the only child of a single mother, I slowly found out over the years what the rest of her family already knew: that she was emotionally needy and an unfillable pit. At age seventeen, I moved out. I continued to support her while making it clear that I would only do so for another year; you may or may not be able to imagine the guilt I felt when the year was up and she plaintively asked, "What will I do now?"

Although I stuck to my guns and didn't give her another red cent (lo and behold, she went on to get a very well-paying job!), I didn't learn my lesson that time. No, that took until my thirties, when she insisted that I move away from a very good life that I had in a wealthy ski resort town to her big city, where I had lived years before and moved away from for very good reasons. This time I finally said no to my mother. Lesson learned? There are some people you cannot please, no matter how you try.

Then there was the string of abusive relationships of various types and intensities, the worst being the marriage from which I escaped with my life and which earned my then-husband a criminal record. The next fellow was nice enough but a needy alcoholic; as I was getting stronger, I realized that the union was sucking the life out of me. The last gent was very good at making me feel like everything was my fault, even the fact that he stole my car! The lessons learned here, however, were not to "stay away from relationships," but to watch out for patterns that you may be repeating and avoid them.

Clearly, I was experienced in romantic relationships, but my loner childhood contributed to my lack of understanding of platonic ones. I was slow to reach out to people I had met in a business school until a classmate asked me to appear on her award-winning ADHD podcast, which garnered me several new clients almost immediately. Lesson learned? Chance encounters can change your life, so it's important to be open, receptive, and alert to those possibilities.

Apparently I had a reputation for being nice to people and easy to talk to, so people weren't afraid to send me referrals. Lesson learned? It really is true that it's not *what* you know but *who* you know that counts—and more importantly, how you treat them. To partially quote Maya Angelou, "People will never forget how you made them feel."

My first virtual assistant had also attended the same business class, and we got on famously for over two years. She patiently (well, not always!) walked me through the vagaries of bulk emails, website design, and many other things required to promote oneself in this digital world, but then I felt that something was changing. As my star was rising, hers wasn't. The jealousy that I sensed from her was borne out by late projects, unresponsiveness, and occasional flat-out rudeness. With sadness I terminated our partnership, having no idea how I would ever do the weekly graphics, let alone bulk emails. I now, among many other things, publish a daily newsletter and produce all of my own graphics. Lesson learned? You never know what you can do until you're forced to.

A seemingly unrelated corollary occurred during that same time period; I noticed that my father wasn't the supportive and helpful cheering section that he had been when I started my coaching career. Spending hours helping me shoot videos gave way to praising the virtual assistant's layouts and completely overlooking the fact that I was the one writing the content, without which there could be no layout. I started to refrain from sharing with him anything that was happening in my business. Matters came to a head when I got brave and told him of the record-setting month I'd just had, only to be met with dead silence followed by a caustic comment.

Lessons learned from these combined incidents? If you are not feeling supported in your endeavors, you're being dragged down, and you may have to terminate, or at least distance yourself from, the relationship. And for heaven's sake, stop looking for approval from these people!

I could go on to include the joy of trading my general holiday angst for helping my new immigrant neighbors to celebrate their first Christmas, but I think you get the idea. This constant evolution can be perplexing, but as I write this, I realize how full my life has been.

The best part of all of these experiences is that I can apply everything I've learned through my life's evolution to my clients' current or potential pitfalls and gently guide them down a different path. They may not always take my advice; some go merrily on their way and then come back later to say, "You were right, Kitti." Frankly, though, I'm less concerned about being right than I am about helping people to create their own turning points in life's learning process; this will help them to pass on that wisdom to others, and the cycle will continue long after I'm gone.

Lauren Archibeque

Lauren Archibeque is a bestselling author, speaker, and trainer with decades of experience. She is an expert at clearing her clients' subconscious of beliefs that are not beneficial and bringing them back to brilliance. Schedule a Begin the Shift call to see if she is your next best step.

www.thegrowthcompany.net

REALLY?! THAT IS NOT MY BEAUTIFUL LIFE

Lauren Archibeque

As I dangle my feet off a cliff overlooking one of the most beautiful canyons in Utah, I am filled with gratitude. Driving the White Rim Trail has been a thrilling adventure. More than one hundred miles of dirt road in the quiet. Navigating sheer drop-offs with inches to spare. Climbing over boulders with no idea what would appear on the other side. Camping under the immense sky with no city lights to mute the spectacular show of stars above. Hours of solitude followed by hilarious evenings of friendship and food. "What an amazing life I get to live!" I said to myself. "How did I get here?"

The road I had traveled was steep and rocky, with deeply carved ruts that threatened to lock me in. Breaking free has had its share of scary moments along with years of searching.

According to the medical community, I should not have been able to experience any of this. Their prediction was that by this time in my life, I would have been permanently disabled for more than three decades and confined to a wheelchair.

In my mid-twenties, I was in a car accident. My car was demolished from behind by a distracted driver. While I walked away from the accident, the following morning I was unable to move my body. I went to the emergency room. I had all the tests they recommended. No broken bones, no concussion. I was told that with muscle relaxants and pain drugs, I would be just fine within a week or two. This was not to be, however.

As the weeks unfolded, I found myself in excruciating pain. Along with body and joint aches, headaches began to plague me daily. I consulted doctor after doctor and submitted myself to test after test. They called the headaches "migraine-style," but they didn't have a remedy. Prescriptions didn't touch the pain unless I drugged myself into a stupor.

Not working was not an option. I was flying without a net or a nest egg. Not only was I responsible for myself, but I also was supporting my mother. She was battling cancer and completely unable to provide for herself.

I found ways to make it through, such as keeping the lights off in my office, lying flat on the floor when I couldn't manage the pain in my body, and making sure that my environment was as quiet as I could make it. Getting to work early in the morning so there was no one talking to me when I needed to concentrate. Collapsing as soon as my workday was done. I spent at least five days a month in bed with fevers and chills.

It was not much of a life. I continued to work with doctors and experts in pain management. I was poked, prodded, and tested for everything you can imagine. No answers. In fact, I was once told that all my symptoms were due to the fact that I was a type A personality. Another doctor referred me to a psychiatrist because I was simply "crazy."

After a few years, I found myself in front of a preeminent pain specialist on the East Coast. He ordered all the tests again. He then sat me down in his office and made his prognosis. He told me that my body was attacking itself, and that there was no treatment. He proceeded to explain that I would never work again. The doctor calmly explained that I would be in a wheelchair by the time I was fifty. Children were out of the question. He handed me a dozen prescriptions and an application for permanent disability.

My brain screamed. My heart hurt. I took the prescriptions and proceeded to spend the next two months in a drug-induced haze. I cried. Then I cried some more.

It's often said that God will never give you more than you can handle. I couldn't help but wonder if that was true. What was He thinking?

This was NOT my beautiful life!

I woke up one morning really angry. Angry at the unfairness. Angry at my body. Angry at the doctors. Angry at life. I let myself fall into self-pity. I allowed myself to wallow in all the things I had already been through in my life.

My childhood had been filled with abuse, poverty, and abandonment. I had been told by a therapist that, based on my childhood, I "should" be a drug-addicted prostitute living in a gutter. At the time, I laughed.

As I sat wallowing in my pain, I realized I had survived all of that. That thought led me to wonder, *How? Why? Why did I survive?* Then the strangest feeling came over me, and in that moment, I knew how I'd survived: I questioned everything!

That was the "how." I never took anything at face value. I asked questions until I found an answer that worked for me—no matter what.

So I began to question myself. I became a detective searching for clues.

I asked myself:

How had I gotten here?

What was I believing that needed to be questioned?

How would I move forward if I were brave?

Where were the answers I needed?

That day became the turning point. I began to seek those answers on my own. I stopped taking the narcotics. I searched and studied any alternative modality that appeared in my world. I began studying Reiki, biofeedback, nutrition, exercise, acupuncture, and homeopathic medicine.

After a few months, I noticed a difference—I experienced one day without a headache. It felt like I had found heaven. The aches and pains were subdued, and I stayed the course—it was working!

A whole new world opened before me. My physical condition continued improving. The only piece still left untouched was the quality of my sleep. I had only been sleeping in short increments that totalled less than four hours a night. Physically there was no reason for this problem. I had to look in a different direction.

It was time to take a deep dive into my brain and my thoughts. The subconscious became my obsession.

I began reading everything I could find. Deepak Chopra, Ken Keyes, Eckhart Tolle, and more. I watched movies over and over: *The Secret*, *What the Bleep Do We Know?*, and others. I joined groups; I attended seminars and trainings like a junkie. This changed every aspect of my life. I began to really understand on a deep level that the answers I was seeking are all on the inside.

All that inner work paid off.

Today, I am not only healthy—I am thriving. I am a proud mom of three beautiful children. I have been an entrepreneur for decades with multiple businesses to my credit. I love supporting others on their path to passion and freedom from the inside out. And there is no wheelchair in sight for me.

Today, I am living fully and completely on purpose. I have gathered over two dozen certifications along the way—including being double-certified as a master

NLP practitioner, hypnotherapist, coach, and trainer. I continue to read, study, and certify to get results—not only for me but for the humans I am committed to serving.

I believe that every soul on the planet has been endowed with gifts for a purpose bigger than themselves.

I believe that limiting beliefs stop most people from fully realizing the fullness of life.

I believe we can all have passion, freedom, and the abundance life has to offer when our internal programming is realigned to support our purpose.

I am grateful for that accident and the gifts it gave me. All the trials and tribulations of my life serve me today in working with my clients. I know the Universe maneuvered me brilliantly into the work I do now.

You do not have to spend decades figuring it out. Days of quiet desperation can be over. Allow yourself to truly shine in all your brilliance. No matter what you are going through at this moment, know that you are divine, you are here for a purpose, and you are loved. May you find your way through the desert and discover the beauty and joy of your life.

Shiraz Baboo

Shiraz Baboo is an award-winning author, international speaker, and reality interventionist. He coaches people to get out of "reality addiction," and his book *How to Rewrite Reality* has changed lives across the globe. Shiraz helps clients to annihilate their unconscious addiction to struggle and lack, resulting in greater free time, money, and energy.

www.energeticmagic.com

THE PROBLEM WAS ACTUALLY THE SOLUTION

Shiraz Baboo

When I was twenty-two years old, I was in university, in the best shape of my life, studying to be a doctor, and the world was my oyster. But the world didn't give me pearls. It gave me arthritis.

I don't mean the "my shoulders are kinda sore" kind of arthritis. I mean pain in every single joint in my body. There were nights when I would sip my dinner through a straw because my jaw was so swollen I couldn't move it. There were days when I couldn't walk because the cartilage between my ankles and shins had worn away, and the bones were grinding against one another.

Now, you may not have been through this kind of physical pain, but have you ever been in a situation with everything planned out, and then *bam!* that plan is gone, and you're left scrambling? If so, I feel you.

You know the emotions that come with it: anger, frustration, despair, self-judgment, self-pity. You ask yourself:

- "What did I do to deserve this?"
- "Why is this happening to me?"
- "What am I supposed to do now?"

Of course, I tried different things to relieve the pain: medication, supplements, diet, even acupuncture and yoga. Someone suggested magnets. And here's the thing: Everything worked ... for a little while. But then the arthritis would come back again with full force.

I built up a pain tolerance that allowed me to get a job. To everyone else, it looked like I moved funny because I was in a little bit of pain. But often the pain was intense. As anyone with arthritis knows, it takes two to ten times as much effort to do any task, so I would tire quickly.

I remember being in a meeting and someone arrived late, complaining that his back was sore from playing sports on the weekend, so he had trouble getting started. A bunch of people expressed their sympathy while I sat quietly in constant pain.

Have you heard people with way better circumstances than you complaining about how hard they have it? And you knew that if you ONLY had to deal with what they did, you'd blow right past them? If you have, then you know how I felt.

So, this became my life. It wasn't until almost twenty pain-filled years later that I met the man who would change my perspective on how reality itself worked.

I had flown to India to meet him, and because it was India, I thought he was going to do some sort of Reiki or laying on of hands and say, "Heal, Shiraz. Heal!" But that's not what happened. He sat down and talked to me every day for two weeks. He was kind of like a psychiatrist, only he wasn't trying to solve anything; he was just gathering information.

At the end of the two weeks, he told me, "Shiraz, here's the problem. You believe you're responsible for everyone in your life."

"No, I don't," I replied.

"I know you don't think that consciously, but from everything you've told me, you formed the belief that you need to be responsible for everyone, and it started when you were eight years old."

"Okay, I know I'm a responsible person, but I don't think I'm responsible for everyone—and what's this got to do with arthritis?"

"Ah, you don't want to be responsible for everyone."

I rolled my eyes. "Yeah. Duh."

"And when you're lying in bed in pain, you don't have to be responsible for anyone, and you don't have to feel guilty about it; when people see you're struggling just to get through the day on your own, they won't ask you to take care of them. It's the solution to a problem you don't even realize you have."

That knocked me off balance mentally. "That's messed up," I said.

"But that's what most illnesses are," he replied. "Solutions for problems people don't realize they have."

Have you ever felt sick of all the responsibilities in your life? That was literally my life.

I thought about what he told me and then said, "Okay, if this is true, then all I have to do is say I'm not going to be responsible for anyone but me, and I won't have arthritis anymore."

He nodded. "Yes—IF you believe it deep down, then you won't need the arthritis."

I gathered my will and said, "I'm not going to be responsible for anyone but me."

And you know what happened in that moment? *Nothing*.

But when I woke up the next morning, I had no pain, no inflammation. I had more mobility, and I could even breathe better.

I was freaking out, though, because this doesn't happen. You don't get rid of eighteen years of illness overnight. And yet I did. Now, the damage done to my body was still there. This is an important lesson: Sometimes you get miracles, and sometimes you get a journey. But if you're not willing to have the journey, you don't typically get the miracles. When you're willing to have both, you tend to get more miracles. Losing the arthritis was a miracle. The restoration of my body has been a journey—one I'm happy to be on.

Are *you* willing to go on a journey filled with miracles?

There was a track that I walked on every day, doing my "old-man shuffle" while others jogged and walked past me. Even people in their sixties and seventies would pass me. That day, I was passing everybody. I was weaving in and out, and they were looking at me with expressions of "What the hell?"

I smiled back with an expression of "I know, right?"

When I got home, everyone was equally amazed. I wasn't limping. I was moving faster. I didn't tire quickly. Everything was just better. And get this: NOBODY asked me to be responsible for them. I mean, why would they? It was a belief created by an eight-year-old.

And this gets better. When I looked more into what happened, I discovered that it wasn't just about illness. It's the reason you don't have the money you want. It's why you don't have the relationships you want. It's why you don't have the clients you want.

You see, your mind prioritizes the avoidance of emotional distress over physical circumstance. It doesn't care about the physical; you do. And the three biggest emotions your mind tries to avoid are guilt, shame, and heartbreak. Arthritis was preferable to the guilt (unfounded as it was) I believed I'd experience.

If you're worried you might feel shame for living a life of abundance while others are suffering, then your mind will make sure to limit your income. And I want to make this clear: It's not if you KNOW you'll feel shame. It's if you think you MIGHT feel it. That's enough to trigger a physical response of "make less money."

Let's saying you're making $100,000 more each year. Are you okay if people start saying things like:

"Can I have some?"

"Can you invest in my business?"

"You need to take care of the whole family now."

"Are you using your wealth to help the poor or are you one of those rich, greedy jerks?"

If you had an emotional reaction to any of those questions, then you are unconsciously limiting your income.

Every consistent physical problem you're dealing with is actually the solution to an emotional problem you're not seeing. And often it's a problem you don't want to see. This is important because it means that it can be impossible to solve this problem on your own. You need someone else to spell it out for you. That's why every physical solution I had for my arthritis eventually failed. It had to. The longer that solution (drugs, diet, etc.) worked while I had the belief I had to be responsible for everyone, the guiltier I felt for only being able to help some people and not everyone. When I let go of the guilt, I let go of the problem.

So, when you deal with the actual emotional problem, the physical problem can just magically disappear. It won't always. You may come up with a physical solution to the problem that finally works, but the timing will line up with when you solved the emotional problem.

Today, I am living the life of my dreams: traveling every month and hanging out in exotic places with amazing people; healthier than I've been in years; and regularly attracting bigger, better opportunities!

Furthermore, when I work with others, doing belief shifting similar to what my mentor did with me, I've been able to get results with people in as little as five minutes. I've helped clients increase their income by ten times, get out of illness, find the love of their life, even fill their events. Imagine how different your life could be if you dropped a limiting belief every five minutes!

Cyndi Barnard

Cyndi Barnard is a Christ follower, wife, mother of three, and grandmother of two. She grew up in southern Indiana where she was a hairstylist for seventeen years before marrying at the age of thirty-six. She is a John Maxwell Certified Team Member and a Life Mentoring School Certified Coach.

www.proverbs31goddess.com

A PLACE TO GROW AND THRIVE

Cyndi Barnard

In 1866 Caroline Dunwoody wrote, "It is my belief that the housewife makes the home, and the home makes the nation."

I like to think I've become a lot like her now.

I just returned from celebrating a wonderful Thanksgiving week together with all my children and grandchildren. We spent Thanksgiving in Orlando this year on account of our eight-year-old granddaughter's cheerleading competition being held there that week. The kids and grandkids spent most days at Disney World while my husband and I stayed back at the condo, chatting with each other and making snacks for when everyone else returned in the evening. My daughter-in-law and I managed to make a pretty good Thanksgiving dinner, and we even celebrated our grandson's seventh birthday.

It made me appreciate how much my family had grown (both physically and emotionally) since this all began twenty-nine years ago.

Because of course, it wasn't always this way. And if you could see the version of me that started this journey, you might suspect I had been replaced by a calmer and more collected clone somewhere along the way.

This story begins with a true whirlwind romance: I met my soulmate in my mid-thirties, and we got engaged after dating for only *three weeks* (when you know, you know). Three months later, we were married, and ten months after that I gave birth to twin boys. In the span of thirteen months, I'd gone from being a single hairstylist—footloose and fancy-free—to being a happily married stay-at-home mom with twins.

It seemed almost surreal. To become a hairstylist back in the 70s, I had to go to school for ten months and then complete 1,500 hours of supervised on-the-job training to get my beauty license. To become a wife, all I had to do was say, "I do." And that's about all I had to say to become a mother. I thought I knew a lot about running a house and taking care of children; I'd been babysitting my nieces for years, and I hadn't starved to death on my own, so I must have known how to cook. It's a common refrain that nothing can *truly* prepare you for becoming a new wife and mother, but I sure wish I'd known a few more of the things I know now than I did then. I was a young Christian at the time, so at least I knew that God was on my side, but things definitely got off to a rocky start.

I've seen friends whose great-grandmothers wrote out all their life lessons in a book that then was passed down through the generations—pages filled with wisdom gleaned from decades as wives and mothers. My great-grandmother didn't do that, but my mother-in-law did give me a book by Emily Barnes that I still treasure to this day, along with a passion for cooking for her son, my new husband. With the internet still in its infancy, I couldn't just pull up YouTube videos on how to efficiently clean and organize a house or get meals on the table when money is tight and the kids are clamoring for attention. I did have some church friends who were gracious enough to help out, but they were all busy with their own lives as well.

Both of my parents worked when I was growing up, and my experience around the house was laundry piled up on the couch, making my own breakfast (mostly cereal) before rushing off to school, and eating cafeteria lunches at school. My dad would get home before my mom and make a can of soup or heat a frozen potpie. (Fortunately, this was toward the start of the TV dinner craze, and I was able to make something to eat even if I was on my own.) As a young girl navigating her way through Catholic school, I knew that something was missing in the house, and I knew that whenever I had kids, I wanted them to grow up with lots of warm fuzzies to remember from their childhoods.

Like most young families, money was tight around the house after our twin sons were born. Things got even tighter when our daughter was born sixteen months later. My husband was starting a new business, and it led us to move far away from all our family and friends. However, that business was too small to pay the bills on its own, so my husband started working a second job driving forklifts at night, leaving me to care for our three children (all under two years old) for eighteen-plus hours a day. With no support network of friends in our new town and the nearest family hours away, I felt very isolated and overwhelmed.

There was a moment—which I remember as if it were yesterday—when I was standing in the kitchen of our shabby old shoebox of a house, staring at a sink full of dirty dishes after feeding my kids, and I just broke down.

I collapsed on the couch, sobbing. These weren't tears of joy or sadness; they were tears of hopelessness and despair.

It seemed like the other moms were "doing it all," while I could scarcely keep our home clean and the kids fed—never mind helping my husband to keep the lights on!

I felt like I had somehow failed at life and things were never going to get better. I called my husband at his office and started crying again, feeling intensely overwhelmed, helpless, and alone. Deep down in my heart, I knew God was still there, but man, He was sure hard to see!

Fortunately, my husband is one to get plugged into a community quickly, and he got me signed up to go on a short church retreat three days later. Those few days of reconnecting with my Savior and feeling treasured by my fellow Christians started me on my recovery with a renewed sense of hope and purpose.

I soon got connected with some other moms who could share homemaking tips (and a glass of Chardonnay).

I started buying cookbooks, took some cooking classes at the KitchenAid store, and found some super-awesome homemaking "gurus" to learn from.

Just a few years after my breakdown, I had become organized and confident enough to pull our children out of school after 9/11 and homeschool them until they entered high school (when we moved to a better, safer school district).

Those children are all grown now. One is working in professional theater, one is pursuing his master's degree at Harvard, and one has started a beautiful family of his own. I guess I didn't mess them up too badly.

I don't want any new wife or mother to ever feel as alone and ill-prepared as I did—that sucked!

I've learned that—apart from the emotional dynamics of operating in a family unit—creating a home is like any other career. It takes a lot of heart and hard work, careful planning, gratuitous budgeting, and being able to think quickly on your feet when things don't go as planned.

In most new jobs, you have a supervisor who can give you on-the-job training and steer you in the right direction. On-the-job training for a young wife or mother is a very independent activity. Schools have largely abandoned any curriculum that resembles what we used to call home economics or personal finance, compounding the difficulty for a new generation of women embarking on one of the most important professions in the world with little-to-no practical education. (And the growing number of stay-at-home dads aren't any better equipped either.)

In Miriam Lukken's marvelous book *Miss Dunwoody's Excellent Instructions for Homekeeping*, Caroline "Big Mama" Dunwoody writes to her children:

I wish for you to understand the larger issues of homekeeping—creating an environment in which all family members grow and thrive, a place where each member may evolve to the full extent our Creator intended!

I am out to continue her mission.

I want to give keepers of the home a powerful head start (or restart), whether newly married or adding a new young one to the family.

Evan Barnard

Evan Barnard, CFP®, EA, has been educating private investors and business owners on the basic, yet vital, principles that must be present in any sound financial situation since 1991. Besides being active in his church community, he facilitates international transformation workshops with the Maxwell Leadership Foundation. He and his wife, Cyndi, reside in Tennessee.

www.pursueyouramericandream.com

FROM THREE STRIKES TO HOME RUN

Evan Barnard

Working in a billion-dollar investment firm serving multigenerational clients is incredibly gratifying. Few things bring me more joy than helping proud parents pay for their kids' college and seeing those children grow up to be productive citizens of our great country, receiving a postcard from a client taking their first vacation as a new retiree, or helping someone who has lost a loved one to navigate the rough waters of grief and inheritance. These are some of the many steps we take to fulfill our American Dream. You could say I built my American Dream by helping others achieve theirs.

Equally rewarding to a fulfilling work life is the financial freedom and free time to enjoy my children and grandchildren, travel the world with my wife, teach transformational leadership in developing nations, and spread the joys of entrepreneurship and capitalism. I love experiencing new things all over the world and being able to bring new concepts back to my clients.

When I started working in financial services with a large national planning firm, it was already my third career. I had previously served several years as a Marine Corps infantry officer, followed by a couple of years doing operational consulting for rapidly growing small and medium-sized businesses in the United States and Canada.

Business started out okay—really more than okay because I quickly became a member of a team practice managing around $85 million. However, I soon became curious about why it seemed that only our company had the right products to solve my clients' problems. I felt like I was being held captive by the products our company was offering to our clients.

I was equally curious about why my clients didn't seem to be doing as well financially as they were supposed to be doing by using the investments I was selling them. I was doing fine, but they weren't. At first, I thought it was because I didn't have enough choices to offer them.

This was during the infancy of the internet. Suddenly there was all kinds of information at my fingertips, with solutions that seemed like they would be better for my clients than what I had access to in my company's portfolio. So I went independent, starting over again and leaving a fair amount of money on the table because of a non-compete agreement. **Strike one.**

I thought the problem was that I couldn't offer my clients the products that would help them the most. If I just had a more extensive menu to choose from, things would be great, and my clients would begin enjoying the success they deserved from their investments. This illusion was perpetuated by my years of sales training from the industry's in-house training gurus.

Now that I was an independent advisor, I had numerous investment companies clamoring for my attention to show their latest and greatest mutual fund. A mutual fund company would have a fund with an excellent three- or five-year track record. Then their wholesalers would descend on us, telling us how great this manager was or how it would be the perfect investment for my client. But all too often, shortly after I had encouraged a client to invest in a particular fund with a great track record, the fund manager went brain-dead or had some other excuse for not performing as well as the market in general. **Strike two.**

Clearly, having a broader selection of investments to choose from wasn't accomplishing what I wanted. I was in a profession where my performance, not my effort, drove my income. Losing faith in what you're doing isn't a great performance enhancer. As a result, my business started to slow down.

Then 9/11 happened. If you recall, the financial markets shut down for five days. That's a long time to be on the beach when you work on commission! We were already operating on a thin margin, and that broke the bank. Nothing I tried worked. The major brokerage firms couldn't pick the right investments, but I hadn't done any better. I was feeling frustrated and hopeless.

Miraculously, the following month—October 2001—a well-known national research firm introduced its own portfolio solution for advisors. Finally, I could harness their expertise in choosing the best investments, allowing me to concentrate on caring for my clients and growing the company. Six weeks after putting my first client into their program, I got an email informing me the firm was replacing one of the funds in the portfolio with a new one with better performance. Seriously, after only six weeks. I wondered why they hadn't used the fund a year ago since it was going to perform better. **Strike three.**

That is when I knew *it wasn't me*; it was *the industry* that was dysfunctional. I had to get out! I couldn't continue to profit from a morally bankrupt system with my clients paying the price. So I started searching for solutions outside the traditional retail brokerage world, and I studied everything I could find on portfolio management. All the while, I was doing everything I could to keep my business going and keep my family fed. I started driving a forklift at night and even temporarily served as an adjunct corporate finance lecturer at the local university.

As the saying goes, when the student is ready, the teacher appears. I responded to an ad in a finance journal about an academic method for building a portfolio. In addition to the Nobel-prize-winning investment strategies I learned, my most significant discovery was how investors' behavior and psychological biases play a crucial role in their investment success. Unfortunately, brokers and advisors are subject to the same biases, and those biases can be as big a part of the problem as a bad investment itself.

Over the years, my eyes have been opened to many myths that the industry perpetuates. Better yet, I learned solutions that actually lined up with the academic finance giants to truly help clients achieve their dreams and goals. One of the hardest things to deal with was acknowledging that I was part of the problem. Yes, the truth will set you free. I haven't looked back, and I haven't changed how I help clients since 2003.

I thought that what I was learning would catch on and become a widely accepted investment standard, but the industry seems to have actually gotten worse. Day-trading in traffic on a phone app, cryptocurrency speculation, 24/7 financial news channels, Reddit groups giving stock-picking advice: It's all chaos. One doughnut won't wipe you out if you're on a diet, but it only takes one mistake to ruin years of work and savings, potentially destroying your future.

I've learned that just because something is widely believed doesn't make it true. You can have all the right tools, but you'll never accomplish anything without action. If you don't understand why your portfolio was built a certain way—or more importantly, if you don't have the discipline to control your behavior through challenging times—you can (and likely will) self-destruct.

Building portfolios using empirically tested, Nobel-prize-winning academic investing principles and combining them with a lifelong coaching relationship to keep your instincts and emotions in the back seat is what I do. Zig Ziglar often said, "You can have anything in life you want by helping enough other people get what they want." My mission is to create confident investors who are empowered to passionately pursue their American Dream. It continues to be an honor and privilege to see my clients do just that!

Jen Beck

Jen Beck is a speaker, author, and founder of Complete Health Revolution with twenty-plus years of experience in physical transformation, mindset, and emotional intelligence development. As a Registered Nutrition Consultant and L.I.I.F.T. UnTherapy Practitioner, Jen coaches leaders to create a vision for their life, master physical and mental health, and achieve any and all dreams.

www.completehealthrevolution.com

THE UNDENIABLE TRUTH ABOUT HEALTH

Jen Beck

When you have your health, you can achieve a thousand dreams. When you don't, you achieve none!

At just twenty-six years old, this became an undeniable truth for me.

It was an average Tuesday. I had just finished my Jr. Bacon Cheeseburger from Wendy's and was still sipping my Diet Coke when my phone rang. It was my older brother, Eric.

I stared at the phone for a second and thought, *What is this about?* We were not close, and he very rarely called. Feeling that tug of worry in my stomach, I answered.

His voice was solemn. "Hey, Jen. It's time."

"Time for what?" I responded.

He quietly muttered, "It's time for Mom to go to a nursing home."

I held my breath.

"What? She's only forty-nine years old!"

I was stunned.

He replied, "She fell out of her wheelchair and got stuck under it in the bathroom. The fire department had to break in to get her out. She's back in the hospital for now, but she cannot go on like this. We have to do something and do it now."

My mom had had multiple sclerosis for over twenty-five years, but she had been independent until this point. She had been on medications to prevent her from having any major relapses. Over the last six weeks, she had gone from being self-sufficient to needing a nursing home. From being able to walk to being 100 percent wheelchair-bound.

Over the course of the next four days, my brother toured over fifty nursing homes. He found the "best" out of all of them. Because she didn't have long-term care, or any retirement savings, she was reliant on Medicaid. The nursing home was not somewhere I would ever choose to place a loved one, but our options were limited, and at least she wouldn't be at risk anymore.

The day we spent sorting through her possessions to decide what would go to her new 8'x10' room, Goodwill, storage, or the garbage was a huge wake-up call.

She clung to every possession, not wanting to let it go, because each represented another piece of her freedom, her independence, and the life she was giving up.

At forty-nine years old, she was way too young to have to do this!

That day, I vowed two things:

1. I had to do something to help Mom, because obviously the "preventative" medications the doctors had her on were NOT working.
2. I had to make some changes, because I never wanted to end up where Mom was, especially given that my grandma also had MS and had suffered greatly.

But how?

I had zero medical background whatsoever. I was a full-time college student with a full-time job.

I had no nutrition background and lived on fast food, sugar, caffeine, and Lean Cuisines.

I started to look for answers. I researched how to be healthy, alternative health methods, which supplements to take, and anything else that might help.

I attended a conference where a pharmacist taught about the healing benefits of superfoods. During his talk, he mentioned that his wife had had multiple sclerosis for twenty-six years.

Following his lecture, I saw the two of them walking across the ballroom. She was virtually untouched. Maybe she had a hand on his arm for stability, but that's it. My mom, on the other hand, had been using a cane since I was seven or eight years old.

I was floored.

I had a chance to meet this woman, and the first words out of my mouth were, "What drugs are you on? Your results are so much different than my mom's, and she needs to be what you are on."

You can imagine my surprise when she said, "Oh, I'm not on any medications. My husband doesn't believe in them."

"Wait. What? Your husband, the pharmacist, doesn't believe in medications?"

She went on to say, "He felt the population studies were too short and the side effects were too great and almost outweighed the benefits."

"So, what did you do?" I asked.

She replied nonchalantly, "I just built up my body with diet, supplements, and exercise."

I walked away thinking about my mom's lifestyle. It was *very* different from Dr. Susser's wife's lifestyle.

My mom never exercised and had taken supplements for only six months when I was in sixth grade. As for meals, we had a wide variety of Hamburger Helper, Tuna Helper, frozen dinners, and canned meals. My mom did the best she could to give us balanced meals, but much of it was processed or nutritionally lacking.

I pondered, *What if Mom had done what Dr. Susser's wife did? Would her results have been different?*

With that thought, I dove into research, trying to find out if nutrition and lifestyle choices really had that much to do with disease progression. The more research I did, the more proof I found that it did.

I read about people reversing MS, heart disease, diabetes, Alzheimer's, fibromyalgia, and just about every other diagnosis that I previously thought of as a life sentence, just by changing their diet and lifestyle.

This is what prompted me to go back to school to become a Registered Nutrition Consultant. I knew I needed more education, because the only lifestyle change experience I'd ever had was trying to lose weight on fad diets.

Fad diets usually meant overhauling everything in one day to fit someone else's idea of what was "right" for me. It meant remaining on the diet until I lost the weight—only to have it all come back a couple of months later—or slipping into the guilt, shame, and self-abuse cycle every time I ate something I "shouldn't" according to whatever plan I had been following at the time.

After my certification, I now had the textbook knowledge to help my mom, myself, and others. I had not yet mastered the implementation of that knowledge, though.

There were lots of trials and errors along the way. Cooking was still incredibly intimidating, so I started by making small changes.

My first step was simply drinking more water.

The increase in energy and alertness I felt seemed almost miraculous. That spurred me on to try another change.

Next I began to eat more fresh foods instead of fries and fast-food burgers and fried chicken sandwiches. That meant Jimmy John's and Panera instead of Wendy's or McD's. Fast-forward, I now cook and eat three healthy, delicious meals each day.

Baby Steps!

Strategic baby steps are the key. I found they move you along the path to your goal and lead to sustainable change. Changing everything at once sets you up for failure.

When you overhaul everything in one day, your brain fights you. It wants to stay safe in your comfort zone, regardless of how uncomfortable it really is. In your comfort zone, where you are right now, your brain knows it can survive. It knows that because you are already surviving.

But what happens when you decide to make a change, any change? It panics!

If you decide to begin drinking the recommended amount of water, which is one-half your body weight in ounces daily, it starts ranting at you. "What? I can't drink that much! I'll be peeing all the time. What happens if I get stuck in traffic? I can't just get up in a meeting with the board to go pee. I'll be up all night." All of the reasons to stay exactly where you are.

I started by making tiny changes to stretch my comfort zone, instead of blowing it up. Increasing my water ten or twenty ounces at a time, I worked my way up and now unconsciously drink one gallon or so a day. It's important to master one habit and then move on to the next.

With my mom's health, I thought I could have more influence. Unfortunately, the nursing home was not a place to make dietary changes because there were no fresh, nutrient-rich foods available. So, I started her on just one supplement that I could slip into her cranberry juice. Then, once we were able to get her into a group home, I had more influence on her diet.

It took me a few years, but I truly transformed my health and lifestyle. Today I have great health, effortlessly maintain my weight, and have incredible energy without reliance on caffeine or sugar.

Today I get to help my clients create a life they love along with the physical and mental health to live it by sharing all of the tools and life hacks I learned along my journey. It enables them to accomplish in a few months what it took me years to do.

And if you are wondering, when my mom passed just before her sixty-fifth birthday, her nurses and medical team shared that we significantly improved the quality of her life and extended it for at least an extra five to ten years.

Kathleen Carlson

Kathleen Carlson is the founder of Straight Up Executive Consulting for female leaders, a bestselling international author, a speaker, and a facilitator. Kathleen has the gift of insight that couples beautifully with her love for people. With her guidance, clients envision, design, and achieve a life that goes from successful to significant.

www.straightupsuccess.com

YOUR VISION. YOUR LIFE. YOUR WAY.

Kathleen Carlson

I was feeling as though my body had abandoned me as I lay on my living room floor looking up at all the things surrounding me. Every part of my body hurt, my eyes were blurred, my mind was confused, my energy was gone—and I was sick and tired of being sick and tired.

I asked myself, "Did I really work myself into a physical collapse for all this stuff?" More serious and honest questions would follow, and those answers would be uncovered in time.

Just a few days prior, I was heading into our monthly senior staff meeting, something I had done a few hundred times, yet nothing about it felt the same. I knew this would be my last meeting.

The company was in the throes of yet another merger. I was used to living in a constant pressure cooker, but this was over the top, even for us. Everyone was on edge, wondering who would be next to go. Seven territories were reduced to six, and the remaining areas were shuffled. I ended up in a territory that had me on the road four out of five nights.

Over the recent weeks, driving had become more challenging. My arms and shoulders hurt so much that just holding the steering wheel was beyond painful. I was continually cleaning my windshield and sunglasses and wiping my eyes. It was as if I was looking through Vaseline. You would think that would be enough to send me to a doctor, but no, I had more work to do. I was a good soldier, and good soldiers do not call in sick. In fact, ignoring your health for the sake of the company's well-being was a team sport that garnered many accolades.

As I sat in that staff meeting, something in me snapped. I could no longer do this. I decided I was going to the doctor as soon as the meeting ended. I discovered that the long hours combined with the years of nonstop stress not only left me with massive amounts of inflammation flowing through my body, but the retina in my left eye also was torn.

Recovering my physical health took five different specialists and nearly two years. Recovering my mental and emotional state took slightly longer.

Okay, God, you have my attention!

The next day, I called my boss and asked him to replace me. I knew I was in for a long road of healing and did not want my team abandoned to a temporary leader. There was too much at risk, too many lives about to be impacted.

I felt ashamed for being sick as though it were a character flaw. I harbored that shame for longer than I cared to admit. Turns out, I was the lucky one. One of my peers found out that the stomachache he had been ignoring was actually stage 4 liver cancer. Little did I know, there would be more like him to come.

Despite my achievements, what I couldn't do was figure out who I was when all the titles and roles were stripped away. I realized that I, too, mostly knew myself by my roles that either chose me or that I chose for myself, mostly by default.

I continued to question everything I thought I knew about myself. I immersed myself in book after book, self-help seminars, weekend retreats, and high-ticket masterminds. After more than a hundred thousand dollars and lots of certifications, I realized that I had had the answers inside of me all along.

I learned more and grew to understand life and myself more in those couple of years than I think I did in all the years prior.

I now understand, we are created as multifaceted human beings, and ignoring any of the key areas of our life catches up with us—usually when we least expect it or can least afford it.

It's easy to come up with examples of this playing out. Who knows a professional who puts all their energy and time into work "for the family," only to lose it all in divorce?

I learned firsthand what happens when you ignore health warnings because you thought you were irreplaceable. Guess what? The moment they needed to replace me, they did.

It was clear that I had been ignoring some pretty important parts of my life. To sort that out and go on to create a life on purpose, I took a deep dive into answering some critical questions.

These questions were simple in nature yet proved difficult to answer. I would like to share what I discovered as I journeyed through the process.

What is it I really want and why do I want it? I'm not talking about vision boards or SMART goals. This is not a linear question, but rather a deep heart- and soul-level question. It's a question that, once it is asked and answered, has the capacity to impact and improve your entire life.

Once I really knew what I wanted, it became crystal clear what fit in and what didn't. Decisions became easy and guilt-free. I now do things because they are part of my life vision, and even the hard things become easier.

Bottom line: If you don't have a vision for your life, someone will fit you into their vision. People and companies are always looking for supporting characters.

Who do I have to BE to have what I want?

- What are my core values?
- What is my Why?
- How do I want to live?
- How do I want to feel?

I could see that I had been shaped and influenced from birth by my parents, extended family, religion, society, etc. As a result, I learned to want what I was taught to want. And then I began to shape my life accordingly and began to follow along the path "I was supposed to follow." Before I knew it, I was completely submerged in a life I never really planned for myself. I often felt absent from my life or like I never really fit.

What do I have to DO and STOP DOING to have the life I desire?

This is where intention meets commitment. It called into question why I wanted something and if I wanted it enough to do what would be required to have it. It sounds daunting, yet the more clearly the first two questions were answered, the easier this answer came. And the time I saved by *not* doing things was life-changing.

I released things I had spent much of my life thinking I wanted and feeling like a failure because I hadn't achieved them. It turns out I only wanted them because I (or someone else) thought I should.

We are meant to enjoy life as we accomplish the things we want to do. I had that completely backward for most of my life. I was waiting until everything was accomplished, and then I was going to enjoy life.

Today, I allow myself the "permission to pivot." I have goals and tasks to do that include many important and necessary things. I also include plenty of things that are just for fun and feed my soul.

You may be thinking, "You make that seem so simple—just figure out what you want, be who you need to be, do the things to have it—and voila!"

It's not a magic trick, I promise. It's life—your life—and you are 100 percent worth the time.

Female leaders were an oddity in the Fortune 50 corporation I was in for more than thirty years. My responsibilities included managing hundreds of millions in sales and profits and all that went with it. My true love of the job came from mentoring, training, and promoting many successful teams. I believe that no matter what business you are in, if you want long-term success, you need to be in the people business first.

I created Straight Up Success because I learned firsthand the value of mentorship. I believe that with the right support, female leaders will change the world.

You are so much more than a supporting character!

When you allow yourself to connect with what you really want and understand what it takes to have it—and begin to followup with only the right actions for you—then the magic of life can unfold. Your Vision, Your Life, Your Way!

Rachael Channing

Rachael Channing is a heart-centered woman and certified coach. She helps retired men and women to reprogram their subconscious fears and false beliefs about time, money, aging, and health so they can enjoy their retirement and spend more time doing the things they are passionate about and say yes to the adventure of life.

rachiegirl1954@gmail.com

WHEREVER YOU GO, THERE YOU ARE
Rachael Channing

I love stories. And thanks to an amazingly rich and sometimes turbulent life, I have plenty of stories to tell—some I made up to comfort or protect myself, some true, and some not.

At a very young age, as a matter of survival, I instinctively turned to telling little lies to protect myself from being judged. I was pretty convincing, too, often fooling myself.

Throughout my life, the negative emotions and beliefs I had suppressed since my childhood were still festering deep inside my subconscious. They often made an appearance in my daily vocabulary and affected the decisions and choices I made.

Despite my many insecurities and lack of belief in myself, I had some amazing opportunities and experiences. The adventurous part of me wanted to take them all in. I went on a journey of self-discovery. I went on spiritual retreats, sought out counseling, tried medications, attended healing summits, and tried different coaching programs.

I also joined a martial arts studio that taught Qi Gong in the Chinese Shaolin tradition. I attended an introductory class, and within the first ten minutes of doing an exercise called Lifting the Sky, the floodgates of my heart opened, and

I started wailing and sobbing from deep inside my chest, releasing years of pent-up pain and anguish.

I was stunned by the energy that instantly filled the empty space in my heart. I was instantly hooked. I started getting stronger and felt more confident. Eventually I earned my Qi Gong teacher certification.

My passion for life became energized. I began connecting with what I love. My relationships took on a deeper level of commitment. I spent two years learning from my coach and eventually became a certified Dream Builder coach.

During that time, I traveled to many countries and experienced local cultures. I lived abroad in Scotland for a time, and I had wild adventures during my stay in India. I thanked God every day for delivering me from my unhappy self. I fully expected that after my travels I would take on a new coaching career, but God had other plans for me.

I had applied to join the sales team at the Gainesville Television Network (GTN) and got hired for my dream job in broadcast sales, marketing, and promotions. As senior sales executive, my hand was firmly on the pulse of the business world in my community and around the state of Florida. I was a member of the Chamber of Commerce and The Business Exchange, served on the Junior League Advisory Board, was a member of the Professional People In Real Estate, served on the University of Florida UF Friends of Theatre & Dance fundraising board, and was a member of the local Gainesville Women's Network.

The perks of my job were awesome! I was invited to every nonprofit fundraising event in Gainesville, had complimentary tickets to all home sporting events, season tickets to the UF Center for Performing Arts, and much more. I also was on a first-name basis with and had access to the president of our company.

I was very good at my job, and my income and business relationships were proof of that. I lived in a beautiful four-bedroom home and owned three great cars—a BMW, a Caddy, and a Trooper.

I woke up every day and said, "Thank you, God! I love my job. I wouldn't want to work anywhere else." I finally knew who I was. My identity was intact. Or so I thought.

In 2012, the winds of change were blowing at GTN. We had a new sales manager I did not trust, and there was talk of the station being sold to a huge media company. Three years later, the ax dropped, and the station was sold.

I was going to be content retiring after fifteen years at GTN. But before I could even announce my retirement, I received an exciting business offer from a good friend that would take me to New Orleans only ten days after I retired from GTN. It was a "too good to be true" kind of offer, one my ego could not turn down.

In the beginning, the work was really exciting. I was meeting well-known musicians and entertainers, which was such a cool experience for me. I loved the energy of the music and dancing and attending the clubs and going to parties.

After about a month of intermittent training, my friend said, "You are on your own!" All my insecurities I thought were long gone came rushing back. Every time I scheduled a meeting to talk about booking music and entertainment for an event, I would pretend to be someone I'm not, masquerading my insecurities just to make everything work. It was exhausting.

I really did love the music, and it became a big part of my life, but I had no local friends to connect with, and I was lonely. It was difficult to pretend while hanging out with the entertainers that I was happy and having fun. I tried, but I just did not fit in that scene.

What happened? This was supposed to be my retirement time—the happiest time of my life. Instead, I was having an emotional breakdown and becoming quite dysfunctional.

Six months into running the business, I had just paid the band and was leaving the casino around 2:00 a.m. in the midst of a torrential rainstorm.

By the time I reached my car, I felt like a wet, shivering dog. I pulled the visor down to look in the mirror, and the shadows on my face made it seem like I was melting away into oblivion.

I suddenly cried out in anguish, "I feel lost. I am really lost!" I started sobbing and couldn't stop. Staring out the windshield, I said out loud:

"Who am I really?"

"What the f**k am I doing here?"

"I'm such an idiot and a failure that I still don't know myself."

"I hate my life, and I want to go home."

"I miss my family."

"I miss my friends."

"I miss feeling loved."

"I hate living in motel rooms and out of a suitcase."

"My son is getting married soon. and I am not even there to help him."

"God, I'm so scared. Please help me!"

I prayed the Serenity Prayer. At that moment, the choice was made. I knew I was done. Done with working really late hours in seedy neighborhoods, done walking alone unprotected in dark parking lots in the middle of the night, done drinking too much to fit in, done waking up at noon only to do it all over again.

I knew that I needed to turn the business back over to my friend. I was in agony wondering how to tell him. I felt guilty and ashamed, fearful of what he and others we knew would think I was a failure. What's worse is that I saw myself as a complete failure too.

The news came as a big disappointment to him. I realized I could not undo what had been done, but I could do everything in my power with love in my heart to make things right. I had to come to terms and forgive myself. I had to ask forgiveness from my friend for not taking responsibility and telling him I would need a few months to decompress and reflect after a fifteen-year career before jumping into a new one. It took a while to build back our trust in each other, but we are good now.

Life showed me good times and bad times, and in both times, the one thing for sure I could trust and believe in was my higher power: God.

I think of God as my anchor, firmly grounded at the bottom of a very rough sea. When life tosses me about, my anchor is there to keep me from drifting too far off course. I loved growing up in the Judaic culture. At age forty-eight, I became an adult Bat Mitzvah (an inner spiritual state of being responsible for my actions). I proudly identify myself as a Jewish woman, and I'm grateful for the gift of my birthright.

I have learned the importance of letting go of false beliefs and putting myself first. Taking care of myself is taking care of others. Long ago I had a dream of being a coach and speaker. I knew I had a message of love and change and passion that I wanted to share with the world, and God willing, to impact a change in people's lives. Now is my time to make a difference, and this is my purpose. I believe that change for a better self and a better life is possible at any time and any age.

Anna Y.C. Chen

Anna Y.C. Chen, the Business Dharma Coach, helps heart-centered entrepreneurs build better business routines. She also shares her knowledge in leadership, team building, and career development through her book-in-progress, *The Business Tarot: The 22 Archetypes and Their Roles in Business*.

www.fromdreamtobusiness.com

THE PURSUIT OF CRAZINESS

Anna Y.C. Chen

It all started in the icy December of 2005. I was out with my university friends, celebrating the end of the final exams in London, Ontario. As we were ordering our food, I casually told my friends how I bombed one of my exams. It was no big deal.

And then, I got the call. It was Dad.

I quickly gestured to my friends that I had to take this call.

"Hey, Dad. What's up?" I cheerfully greeted him.

Within seconds, my stomach sank. It was Grandpa. He had suffered a heart attack and passed away.

Over the phone, Dad and I quickly settled on a plan for me to leave Ontario right away for Vancouver, BC, meet up with him, and then take another flight together back to Taiwan. Flight time took around sixteen hours, but I didn't care how long the journey took; I just wanted to return to Taiwan and be with my family. I wanted to be back at Grandpa's place as fast as possible!

How could this be? He just had surgery!

I thought he'd be there for my wedding! I had yet to introduce my boyfriend to him! He didn't even see me graduate!

All my dreams with my grandfather in the picture? *Pfft*. Gone. And life went on, whether or not I was ready to let go of my grief.

Just as I was about to finish my semester after Grandpa's funeral, another bell struck. This time, my dad lost his older brother to aggressive cancer.

My uncle and his family lived only two doors from my parents, and I spent many afternoons at his house hanging out with my cousins. In June 2005, my uncle discovered his cancer, but his health rapidly deteriorated between January and March 2006. My parents knew about this and decided not to tell me. I didn't even know my uncle had cancer until my mom told me about his death! He was young, only in his fifties!

Two people in my life were gone within four months. It felt unreal. At that point, life was a big joke to me, and it continued to be ironic.

Another month or two went by after my uncle's funeral. Over the phone, my aunt told me another secret she and my parents were keeping from me: My father had been diagnosed with early-stage thyroid cancer. He was lucky that his cancer was diagnosed early, and Dad received his operation after my uncle's funeral. My aunt reassured me after her confession that "everything looks fine, but your dad needs regular follow-ups from now on to make sure his cancer doesn't come back."

Wait. What? Pause. Time out. Did my aunt just tell me that I could lose Dad, too, after losing Grandpa and my uncle in four months?

That was too much for me to deal with, so I was not surprised when I got diagnosed with depression mid-2006. It explained why I wanted to hide at home most of the time and felt unmotivated to do anything. *Life was a gray muck*, and I was stuck in it.

Since I wasn't attending class, my grade point average suffered and slipped below the program requirement. I got kicked out of the business program but remained in school. My world had been turned upside down. I felt like a failure in life, defeated and embarrassed. For the next few months, I remembered lying in bed for hours, not talking to anyone, yet being fully aware that I could not go on like this.

Some days, I would be angry at God for letting things happen this way, while I spent other days begging for His help. I just needed my old life back! Somehow, I thought my life would be "normal" and happy again if I returned to the business program. So I started my application for readmission and decided to demonstrate my effort in getting my life back on track by going to counseling.

I didn't know if counseling would help at that time or even what counseling was. I thought it was a tool to prove that my depression was getting better. Instead, I found the ugly truth that I could no longer ignore: I was bullied throughout my life and had never healed emotionally. *Great. My life sucks. Now what? What's next?*

As it turned out, counseling showed me the problems but didn't help me solve them. Not knowing where else to turn, I took it upon myself to figure things out. I picked up reading, and it was one of the best decisions I have ever made.

Among the many books I read, one author, Tom Wang, mentioned a Japanese proverb in his book *Stanford's Silver Bullet* [trans.] about how **one needs the courage to jump off the stage of Kiyomizu to become successful.**

Right. It's ONLY a stage. How HARD could THAT be?

Well. As it turns out, the stage of Kiyomizu temple in Kyoto, Japan, is about four to five stories high. According to folklore, if a person is willing to jump off the stage of Kiyomizu, God will grant that person's wish, which, in modern-day words, means wishes will come true when one has the courage and determination to die for something important.

So I asked myself: What was my one thing worth dying for? Then one afternoon, the answer came to me. I remember breaking down in front of my friend, crying, and confessing my deepest desire.

"I want to be onstage! I don't care if I have to sweep the stage floor. I don't care if I have to be a stagehand. I don't care if I have to dance. I don't care! I want to be onstage," I said to my friend.

"And how are you going to do that?" she asked.

"I am going to audition for the Music Faculty at our school," I stated.

"OK, what are you going to major in? Piano?" she asked in confusion.

I glared at her. "No. You know me! I would never major in piano!" I waved my arm in the air and continued, "I want to major in voice!"

There was a moment of silence.

"Are you crazy? You've never taken a single voice lesson before! Plus, our school teaches classical singing. Not pop!"

But I wasn't going to let that stop me. It was my last chance: the make-it-or-break-it moment. At the time, I thought becoming a voice major was my chance to be onstage. My university score was not high enough to audition for music faculties elsewhere—*but* I knew most universities would not turn down an alumna. My school might be lenient if I played my cards right!

Something magical happens indeed when you declare your intentions! This crazy dream to be on stage became my biggest motivation to overcome depression.

With my newfound passion, I managed to sample a few classes from the Music Faculty, get reinstated into my business program, and graduate. In 2007, I passed my music audition after a year of voice training. In exchange for financial support to pursue my musical dream, I promised my parents that I would study for my accounting designation exam while maintaining good grades in my music studies. This meant adding about ten extra hours per week to my music curriculum, not counting practices, rehearsals, exams, and homework.

And I DID IT! Not only did I pass my Certified Management Accountant entrance exam in 2008, but I also graduated with honors in Music in 2011. On top of that, I was accepted into a master's degree program in Choral Conducting and won a full-fledged scholarship in my second year.

Looking back at that crazy period, here are some tips that helped me get unstuck and turn my life around.

1. **Be ready to build new, beneficial habits and routines** because the world will keep generating new circumstances to experience and new problems to solve. We can apply the same solution to the same problem or learn to build new habits or routines to avoid the same problem again. The first option provides temporary solutions, whereas the latter solves a problem from its root. I'd recommend the latter one.
2. **Pursue your dreams, no matter how unachievable they might seem.**

The number-one regret of those on their deathbeds is choosing not to pursue their dream when they had a chance. It leaves people unsettled in their last waking moments, feeling restless over what could have happened. There could be a million reasons not to pursue your dream, but never give it up before taking action to make it come true, because you only get to live once.

I wish you lots of joy pursuing your dream life and business!

"You're entirely bonkers. But I'll tell you a secret. All the best people are." —Lewis Carroll

Jenny C. Cohen

Jenny C. Cohen, Outside In Recovery Coach, presents a multidisciplinary approach (Occupational Therapy, somatic dance, yoga, trauma-aware Neuro-Linguistic-Programming, Reiki) so you can thrive with her Dance to Heal program. She lives in Utah with her family, two dogs, and 12.3 cats.

www.outsideinrecovery.com

ARE YOU LOST AT SEA?
THRIVING AFTER BREAST CANCER

Jenny C. Cohen

In January of 2014, I competed in my first two belly dance competitions. I had been dancing since 2002. I ended up winning and was invited to Germany where I placed second runner-up!

My kids were older, and it felt right for me to start focusing on myself. They were homeschooled all their lives. Because I had them through IVF, they were my miracle babies and the center of my universe for a long time. Since January 2014, after hard work, I was at my pre-baby weight and feeling strong as I neared my mid-forties. I thought I was in the best shape of my life.

Out of the blue, my husband had emergency bowel obstruction surgery that May and was in the hospital for a week. Not only did I stay by his bedside day and night, but I also had two kids sleeping in the car with our two dogs. My son had type 1 diabetes, and it was imperative to check his blood sugar at night just in case he didn't wake up when he hit a low. When his blood sugar level was below forty, he had to wake up to take care of it, but he didn't always do that.

I literally got a couple of hours of sleep each night, completely ignoring my own self-care needs. I only focused on my husband and the kids. I was burning the candle not only on both ends but also in the middle.

At my physical later that month, I said to the doctor, "I found a lump."

He said, "You need to go and get a mammogram right now." I went and had a mammogram, ultrasound, and biopsy. I think that's when I started to really disassociate. In my mind, I thought, *I have things to do, kids to take care of, I'm very busy, and this is in my way.*

And then I got the call.

"You have cancer."

I blinked away the tears in my eyes and put on a brave face. I still kept myself on a back shelf when it came to the kids and family.

When I spoke to my doctor the following week, his words were, "You can't wait. This is dire. If you were my wife, I would be sending you to Memorial Sloan (the top cancer hospital on the East Coast) yesterday."

When I met with the surgeons, they explained to me that my type of breast cancer was triple positive and would require treatment starting as soon as possible and extending through the end of the year.

After the first chemotherapy round, which everyone lovingly called Red Death, we got home, and I remember saying to my husband, "That wasn't so bad." I didn't fully understand how much my body would suffer.

My hair started coming out in clumps around day ten, so I placed a huge, two-hundred-dollar order of Halloween wigs. I made plans to keep doing dance events throughout treatment.

In reality, I was already experiencing some of the hardest things about getting through chemotherapy such as loss of energy, taste, and feeling in my hands and feet.

No one really talks about the surreal feeling of having to sit still, shut down your fight-or-flight reflex, and stay sitting while poison is being pumped into your body—not once, not twice, but repeatedly, even as your body starts to break down from it.

When I started to lose feeling in my hands, fingertips, feet, and toes, the doctors asked if I wanted to stop the chemotherapy.

"Does that mean I don't need it?"

"Oh no, you need it! We just don't want your quality of life to be affected because we know you're a dancer."

"So I have to pick?"

I had to pick between: 1) being healed from cancer while losing pretty much all feeling in my feet and hands, or 2) having a better quality of life but no guarantee I'd get rid of all the cancer.

I chose the first option because I wanted to see my kids grow up, and I wanted to have a full life.

I went through the complete treatment of sixteen chemotherapy rounds, surgery, thirty-six radiation sessions, an additional year of infusions, and six years of oral hormone-blocking medications.

And through it all, I danced.

But something shifted in the way I was dancing.

One day I found myself unable to find myself in the mirror. I was fully dressed and made up, but I couldn't see myself. I could see the outline of the costuming and the outlines of my hair, but I couldn't see my face or my body—it was like my eyes would skirt over my actual reflection. I didn't really acknowledge that I wasn't present. I kept ignoring it and pushing harder to perform and travel more. I kept myself busy and moving. I was going through the motions.

Disengaged. Distracted. Depleted.

I thought I was "being there" for everyone just as I used to be.

I was adrift at sea, completely lost, and not even aware of it.

While on a trip, one of my children told me they were on the verge of suicide and showed me their scars from self-harm. I went into clinical mode. Therapy was set up and all the sharp objects were locked up. I thought it would be okay. But reality found a way of grabbing me and stopping me in my tracks.

Two weeks later, while I was at a local dance workshop, my precious child found a new filet knife I had missed and had a relapse of self-cutting. This immediately brought me back to the realization that I hadn't been present in a long time. I had completely missed all the signs when they stopped talking and withdrew into themselves.

I sobbed as I put butterfly strips on the cuts while my child looked at me with a stranger's eyes, and suddenly I knew the full truth.

My child would not be saved unless I made the choice to be wholly present and in my body.

And thus began my search for ways to be present even though it didn't always feel so safe. Honestly, it's much easier to be lost in the past because that's something you know, or to just seduce yourself into thinking you're in control by planning for the future.

Being present meant that I had to feel my feelings.

Feelings like:

- "Why is everything so hard?"
- "How do I keep everyone around me safe?"
- "It'd be really easy just to give up right now."
- "Why did I survive, and they didn't?"

If you're thinking similar thoughts, you are not alone.

Over the past seven years, I found my way back through the DISCOVER process:

- I confronted the thought "Did I almost die?" and celebrate daily that I lived.
- Moving while being present was part of my true healing because part of the problem after the medical treatment was the trauma freeze response during it all.
- Getting back in touch with feeling content and safe in my body again was another key to thriving.
- Finding and embracing self-love may be a cliché, but it's an important part of how I recovered.
- I let myself feel the rage of everything in my life. And in letting it go, I stopped poisoning myself.
- I am the sum of all my past traumas parts. Finding them all made me whole.
- I worked on my powerful subconscious. "Until you make your unconscious conscious, life will happen to you, and you will call it fate" (Carl Jung).

- I returned to my true self before the world got to me. I started to play. I continued a combination of actions heightened with emotion and resetting beliefs for lasting results.

Today, both my children are thriving, bright-eyed college students on the dean's list with unlimited futures. We save neonatal orphaned kittens together. My beloved husband and I celebrated our thirtieth wedding anniversary. While I am instantly aware of my family's special needs when they need me, I maintain healthy boundaries and have launched my *Dance to Heal* book, program, and podcast. I see my whole self when I dance on my viral Instagram reels. I embrace and love my second chance at life.

After my breast cancer treatment, I felt lost at sea like Rose from the *Titanic* movie.

Today I am transformed into a mermaid, and the sea (my new now) is my fulfilling life and playground.

I invite you and all of your survivor friends to try the DISCOVER process, which I share in my book *Outside In Recovery* available on my website. See and feel your beauty again in your own second chance!

Ramesh Dewangan

Ramesh Dewangan is the founder and CEO of Quantum Vision Consulting, focusing on career and leadership coaching of experienced tech professionals. He is a bestselling author, Distinguished Toastmaster, and a John Maxwell Team certified coach, speaker, and trainer. His online course is now offered as a certificate course by an accredited university in Southern California.

www.quantumvisionconsulting.com

BREAKING OUT OF STRUGGLES AND LEADING YOUR WAY!

Ramesh Dewangan

My life's journey has not been a bed of roses.

My foray into a startup very early in my career failed. My wedding took place during this time, and I had to rush to Germany immediately after the ceremony, leaving my dear bride behind. I didn't get paid for months; we exhausted all of our savings. We didn't have enough money to afford food at a decent restaurant. I frantically looked for a job change and eventually was able to join a high-profile US multinational.

But over the years, I realized that I had become a hardworking professional with no career growth. My colleagues all seemed to be getting ahead in their careers. I had a hard time saying no to more work being dumped on me. I was working on goals one after one. I didn't take many vacations. I couldn't spend time with my family. My manager didn't follow up on promotional opportunities despite my raising the concern several times. I was stressed and overweight. My career had stalled.

A few months later, another painful moment occurred when I had to leave my twelve-day-old daughter behind to travel abroad for work. Mind you, she was twelve days old, not twelve months or twelve years. The travel opportunity for work left me emotionally drained. When I looked into the pleading eyes of my wife, I could see that she was trying to be brave and assure me she would be all right. There was no doubt, though: She needed me, my newborn needed me, and I needed my family. I locked myself in a room for a few minutes and cried. I wondered if the time would come when I could play with my baby after work and be there for my family. I felt I was the unluckiest hardworking employee on the planet.

Once again, I decided to make a concerted effort to change my job. I undertook intensive people skills training and management courses. I took up more cross-functional international projects. I was ecstatic when I got a great job offer from a Silicon Valley technology company based in California—an offer too good to refuse. I waited for a few days before announcing it to anyone until I could convince myself that it was indeed real.

But just when I thought I saw some light at the end of the tunnel, the worst was yet to come. I had to take my young family to Chennai, India, a six-hour train ride from Bangalore, to get a US visa. The entrance to the US consulate was so crowded that we got caught in a huge melee, resulting in the consulate calling the police. The police assaulted the crowd with sticks, and I was afraid my kids (then one and five years old) would be hurt in action. I decided to extract my family from all this and head back home. My determination was beginning to crack.

At the railway station for the train ride back to Bangalore, my wife, and daughter were in the Ladies' Waiting Room, and my son and I were in the adjoining waiting room. Suddenly my daughter came rushing up to me with tears in her eyes, saying, "Mom fell in the bathroom, and she is badly hurt." I rushed to the restroom. My wife had collapsed on the floor and was crying in pain, with several fellow passengers consoling her and trying to help. We would come to find out that she had broken both of her hips.

I panicked as I knew no one in that town. I decided to urgently look for a taxi to take us straight to the hospital in Bangalore.

The first available taxi turned out to be in miserable condition. It could barely pick up speed beyond forty miles an hour, sputtering all along. What should have taken six hours took a total of twelve. My wife sobbed all the way in excruciating pain. My kids were scared, looking at me to fix the situation. Finally, we reached the hospital. My wife was hospitalized for a week, so I had to arrange medical visits with the doctor to see her at our house. It took more than three months for her to recover. Now my determination really took a major hit.

A month later, I received a gift from my US employer with a sweet welcome letter. I felt optimistic about the opportunity. The next day I received a call from someone at the international movers contracted by the hiring company. He asked what household items I would like to move. I said I didn't plan to move anything.

The mover said, "What about your sofa?"

I said, "My sofa is shaking from all angles; it will fall apart if you move it."

Next, he asked, "What about the refrigerator?"

I said, "My fridge is so old and makes such a loud noise I can barely sleep at night. That's the last thing I want to take."

He then agreed that I had nothing to move. I decided to forgo the service. But the call gave me a huge encouragement to make a change.

That did it. I was on a roll all over again. I convinced my family to move, and we went to a different city, New Delhi, to try to get the visa one more time. This time I got the visa within an hour. There was plenty of time left for us before the flight departed. Since most Americans coming to India always visit the Taj Mahal, and we had not seen it, so off we went. That way we could answer if any Americans asked us what the Taj Mahal was like.

That's how my wife and I landed with two kids and two suitcases in hand at San Francisco International Airport twenty-five years ago. I was happy to join the company that gave me a highly fulfilling role. Life was beginning to look up.

After two weeks, I found I had been overpaid by ten thousand dollars in my paycheck. I thought it must be a mistake. I reported this to the finance department. They did a review and informed me that it was the reimbursement for not using the international movers. What the company paid me as the moving cost was more than my entire year's salary in India.

Then, a few months later, I found I had been overpaid by another seven thousand dollars. Again I thought it must be a mistake. The finance department reviewed it and informed me that my employment contract stated I was to be paid ten thousand dollars net for the moving expenses. The seven thousand dollars was to account for the taxes. That was wonderful news and went a long way for me to own my first single-family home within two years of arriving in the United States.

Moving to the States brought a great opportunity for my career advancement, and I was able to take care of my family in ways I couldn't even imagine in India. I took my children to Disney World in Florida for an entire week. I probably enjoyed Disney World more than my own kids. We went to a summer camp deep in the California redwood forest at Loma Mar, where the children had a blast. We did midnight hiking, enjoyed the streams, and sang Kumbaya in the evening with fellow campers.

I decided to join a community leadership program in the city of Cupertino, California. That work helped me connect with the people and bring the community together. I joined Toastmasters, where I developed my communication and leadership skills. I went on to achieve the Distinguished Toastmasters Award, their highest recognition. I also became a district officer of Toastmasters, leading several Bay Area clubs.

I can't forget the sense of joy and achievement when I got promoted within two years at my work to the senior manager position with ten-plus people reporting to me. My father sent a three-word note: "You did it!" My efforts finally paid off, and I felt highly fulfilled by making my parents proud.

In summary, I was stuck at low points several times. I learned lessons and made key changes throughout my career to leap forward. Three core lessons that I've learned are that for career growth with higher income and influence:

No one is born with connecting, influencing, or leadership skills.

A growth mindset is the key.

You must impact the team and the organization with integrity and efficiency for success.

I did it, and so can you!

Sharon Galluzzo

Sharon Galluzzo, Profit Growth Strategist at Profit Connections, is the author of several Amazon bestsellers, including *Legendary Business: From Rats to Riche$*. In her more than eighteen years as an entrepreneur, Sharon has coached professionals across the country from franchisors and solopreneurs to businesses on the verge of expansion.

www.sharongalluzzo.com

THE DANGER ZONE

Sharon Galluzzo

I don't introduce myself to everyone with, "You know, you're doing that wrong," but when I do, he marries me. True story.

Peter and I have been husband and wife for almost three decades now. He is the epicenter of my greatest adventures and my partner in life and business. We have two amazing daughters. We live at the beach with our fur babies, Sugar Plum and Bella. Prior to living the beach lifestyle, we owned a successful business together for more than a decade. Then we sold it... for a profit.

My husband is one of those steady guys. You know the type: even keel, mellow personality, and rock solid.

Funny thing about those rock-solid, steady guys. Sometimes they get stuck. He didn't want to change anything. He was perfectly happy to keep things the way they were. Perfectly happy to date me long after college. Perfectly happy for me to continue to live in his mother's attic. I started calling him Mr. Status Quo.

Frankly, I began to feel like Mona Lisa Vito in *My Cousin Vinny*. "My niece, the daughter of my sister, is getting married!" Well, at least she was engaged to Vinny! It took us six years in total to make it to the altar.

For a better quality of life, we moved from New York to North Carolina. What we created was beautiful. We had two kids, a dog, and a house with a backyard. My husband secured a position and was making a good salary. We had a wonderful, comfortable life, and we were happy. At least I thought so.

Then, out of the blue one day, Mr. Status Quo came home and expressed his frustration. "I feel stuck," he told me. "I want to be more creative, do something else." Then he dropped the bomb. "I want to start a business. I want to be my own boss."

You think you know someone, and then suddenly your introverted, risk-averse, frugal husband wants to spend hundreds of thousands of dollars on a business venture. He wasn't even old enough for a midlife crisis!

I felt my knees grow weak as panic set in. My brain was racing hundreds of miles an hour with so many questions that I couldn't even speak. My thoughts were a jumble. *What? A business? Businesses are risky. What if we don't make any money? What if we lose it all? We have small kids. What will this mean to our life?*

After the initial shock wore off and I could breathe again, I agreed to investigate it with him. You would have thought we were official PIs the way we dug into every nuance of his chosen specialty. Once the investigative stage was completed, we turned to saving money. We got out of debt. Then, finally, it was time. We were ready to take the plunge.

Oh my gosh, we were honest-to-goodness entrepreneurs.

We figured that building a business was a lot like building a house. A house requires architects, carpenters, blueprints, plumbers, electricians—all the experts. So, if we were building a business, we needed to bring in business experts.

We found mentors and asked lots of questions. We invested in coaching and training on how to do "the thing" and, most importantly, how to run a business. I took classes, networked, read books, and learned everything I could. We actually did what our coaches told us to do. (Here's a pro tip: Do what your coaches tell you.) Interestingly, I found I had an aptitude for this business thing.

Letting people know about our fledgling business was paramount. Heaven help you if you were standing in line behind me in the grocery store! "We are opening a business! Here's the info!" Yep. I'm that lady.

In addition to the administrative and marketing side, we planned for and secured cash reserves. One thing we knew was that a generous cushion in the bank was essential, and we had that covered.

We did everything right.

Human adults constantly receive massive amounts of information. For new information to lodge in the brain, on average it takes seven exposures. That means that new businesses must advertise and constantly be in front of customers.

I knew this, so I went big! I rolled up to the publisher of the biggest print magazine in the area. "I want to advertise in your publication. Not just for one town but both. Yeah, and I want to commit to six months in each." We signed the contract. It was expensive, and were are locked in to monthly payments. This was before Facebook Ads or targeted Google searches made advertising more flexible.

Did I mention that it was 2008? Yes, *that* 2008. The Great Recession. Banks were failing. Businesses were closing their doors just as we opened ours.

Then reality hit.

On a random Thursday, I went to my desk as usual. I checked our bank account online and was shocked to see that our balance was just two thousand dollars. "Wait, that can't be right," I whispered as my mind began to spin. Bills were coming due—big ones. Sitting stunned in my chair, I realized I was holding my breath. I released it, and as I inhaled once again, I was filled with the sense of complete dread as I realized I had to tell my husband.

Peter wasn't due home until 6:00 p.m. I felt time taking on a life of its own. Each minute took an hour and yet the hours flew by. Then suddenly the day was over. Feeling sick to my stomach, I heard the key in the lock.

Somehow, I found a way to tell him the news. The words tumbled out of my mouth in a rush. He didn't understand what I was saying or why I was crying. He was confused and pacing around the bonus room where our studio was set up.

"How did this happen?" he asked.

"Of course, he would ask that. Of course, he's right," my mind silently screamed.

Our heated and emotional exchanges went around and around the same refrain. We had invested so much: our time, energy, and especially our money. It dawned on us that our emotions would change nothing. The only thing we could do at that moment was make a choice. Either we could chalk this up to a profoundly expensive lesson and pack it in, or we could make it work.

It was time. Ride or die. Did we have what it would take for the long haul? The thought haunted me that we could be the proverbial gold miner who gave up his claim only to find out later that he stopped digging three feet short of the gold.

Standing there in our studio, which was actually the our kids' former playroom, surrounded by painted clouds on all sides of us, we made a decision. No equivocation.

We *would* make this business work, *no matter what.*

Let me break that down. One, we decided. Two, our business was going to work. Three, we were committed, no matter what. Four, no more trying. It must work.

And it did.

Looking back now, we can clearly see that, even though our bank account was dangerously low, the systems, practices, and strategies we put in place from day one saved us. Our bank account never hit zero. We didn't quit just three feet from gold.

Because of the coaching, spending money on advertising, doing what we were supposed do, and fully committing to the business, as if by magic and all at once, the phone started ringing, customers came in, and we got good at sales. And it never stopped.

We went from less than two thousand dollars to six figures in year two and multiple six figures by year four. We won awards from our community and industry and were in business for more than a decade before we sold it. We walked away on our terms, with profit in our pockets.

Today, I help business owners grow and scale as a Profit Growth Strategist.

Often entrepreneurs waffle between drowning in too much information and too many experts or nothing at all. Then they wonder why success takes so long and why the results are so mixed. When I deconstructed what made us successful, I realized that the key was how we operated.

I'm a strategy maven, so I made sure we had a defined strategy for how we approached everything from the initial research and building our brand to ongoing operations. I don't like cumbersome, so I made them simple. Those microstrategies were the backbone of our success. It was how we could work together as a unit, keep our marriage and sense of humor intact, and reach our goals and dreams.

I thought becoming an entrepreneur was dangerous. I thought risking it all was dangerous. I thought almost going under was dangerous. But I was wrong. The most dangerous place to be was in my comfort zone. Stepping out of it made all the difference.

Michael Hession

Michael Hession is a financial professional specializing in the Infinite Banking Concepts, of which he is an authorized practitioner. Michael works with families and entrepreneurs to help them achieve true financial independence by implementing tried-and-true strategies that the wealthy have taken advantage of for decades.

www.michaelrhession.com

FROM BANKRUPTCY TO FINANCIAL PEACE OF MIND—A TALE OF TRIUMPH AND PERSISTENCE

Michael Hession

If you were to travel back in time with me to early 2007, it might have looked like my wife, Ann, and I were just crushing it, and the world was our oyster!

We had recently sold our two-family property for a nice $100k profit, turned those proceeds into a six-unit multifamily rental unit, and it was fully rented and cash-flow positive.

Annie started a promising online business, and I learned to trade in the stock market and was successfully trading in the equity options space. I'd even made just under seven thousand dollars in one day alone!

Along with our two beautiful young daughters, two dogs, and two cats, we lived in a wonderful older home with a big backyard and an above-ground pool. Our home was a regular gathering place for our kids and friends.

Like so many others, we were soon to be significantly impacted by the "Great Recession of 2008."

Our fledgling business enterprises drew inconsistent revenue, and since the real estate space was the main driver in the economic downturn back then, our six-unit suddenly got a lot harder to keep fully rented and was now losing money.

We were badly overleveraged and started to feel the pinch of our debt obligations. As the broader economy continued to unravel, we grew desperate for a way out. I even borrowed money from a close cousin so I could replenish my trading account to try and keep us afloat. By this time, the stock market had become a volatile and untenable roller coaster. I can still recall being in my home office watching multiple screens, setting up trades that my research revealed to be sound—and then not being able to push the button to initiate the trade due to the overall stress we were experiencing. I'd lost my mojo, for sure.

Our debt got out of hand and our income fizzled away, so we sought help. Initially, we tried working with a lawyer-based debt relief company, where you agree to stop paying your bills and cease communicating with your creditors. I know, it sounds crazy, but the idea is that you instead redirect those funds to the law firm, and eventually they'll negotiate your debts down while you come out relatively unscathed.

I can clearly remember the day one of my daughters came into my office and asked me these two questions: "Daddy, who keeps calling us all the time? And why don't you and Mommy ever pick up the phone?" *Ouch.*

Eventually, a new lawyer assigned to our case reached out to us upon reviewing our numbers and seeing our progress—or lack thereof. Her conclusion was that this was not the best route for us and that we probably wouldn't be able to set aside enough funds to effectively negotiate our debt down after all. Adding insult to injury, she suggested we investigate that dreaded B-word: *BANKRUPTCY.*

"Ugh," was all I could muster at the time.

It was not something that we had even remotely considered, although I'd met and read about some entrepreneurs who wore multiple bankruptcies as badges of honor. It was hard for us to consider that as an option; my shame and sense of failure was complete. I'd become so despondent I considered ending it all in hopes that the term life insurance we had would pay out and at least my family would be taken care of.

But there didn't seem to be any other options, so bankruptcy it was. Ours was discharged in September 2008, with ten years of lousy credit staring us in the face and lots of wound-licking. Honestly, I'm grateful for the lawyer who took the initiative to be straight with us. Better to know where you really are, with a chance to fix it than going down a path with no hope.

The following few years were a humbling reentry into the workforce for me. I hadn't worked for anyone but myself for some twenty years. At age forty-five, I got a job as a chauffeur. I figured hey, I was a good driver, was approaching middle age: and looked pretty good in a black suit!

Around this time, I started to reengage with personal development again, primarily with Landmark Education. I felt so lousy I knew I needed to do something to get out of this funk, so I assisted at Landmark seminars and even volunteered at a local soup kitchen, where I got to see how good I had it after all. Being of service to those in much greater need than me was a powerful experience and informs who I am today.

After short stints as a furniture salesman and Uber driver, I even tried trading again. But my heart just wasn't in it, and I don't like how it's a zero-sum game and the house always wins in the end.

Eventually, I started working for a large life insurance company, Bankers Life. It made sense to get back into the broader financial space since I'd spent so much time learning about and participating in those markets. It was here that my eyes were opened to the depth and power of life insurance—that it is so much more than just money left behind for your loved ones when you die.

There are certain types of life insurance that are legitimate assets, with tax-free, guaranteed growth components built into them that have zero, or limited, exposure to the ups and downs of the stock market. After my experiences with the stock market and real estate, where outside forces can greatly impact whether you win or lose, I loved this idea! The problem with those markets is that it is largely based on these two questions: 1) Did you get in at the right time? and 2) Did you get out at the right time? In the case of our first home, the two-family that we sold for a $100k profit, our timing was awesome . . . barely. We sold just before things started going south in the local real estate market. In the case of the six-unit property, our timing was terrible—we paid top dollar near the top of the cycle, went deep into debt with it, and then suffered the consequences of the real estate bust.

My brilliant bride alerted me to a new client of hers, Tom, who specialized in a similar life insurance vehicle to what I was offering. He had an upcoming podcast that I listened to, and I quickly realized that his approach was superior to what I could do with my current company.

From Tom I learned about something called Infinite Banking Concepts, and our lives were about to change forever. I am eternally grateful to him for planting the seeds and getting us started on our first infinite banking policy, and the rest is history.

- As opposed to being completely at risk in the markets with no guarantees, we could now enjoy guaranteed growth of our money with zero market risk and a consistent high rate of return.
- As opposed to being at the mercy of outside forces we have little or no control over, we have complete control of our wealth.

We could now take advantage of:

- Tax-free and inflation-proof growth of our money
- The ability to turn debt into wealth and outflow of money to inflow of money

- The magic of uninterrupted compounding growth of our money
- The ability to create intergenerational wealth for our children and future grandchildren

As a captive agent with Banker's Life, I could only offer the contracts that they had, and they weren't particularly good.

A week after listening to that podcast, I said to my manager, "Look, I can't keep doing this when I know there's something better out there for people but this company doesn't offer it. I would be completely out of integrity if I stayed. Thanks for the opportunity, but it's time for me to go!"

There were some fits and starts professionally for a few years, but after meeting with my eventual mentor Vance, with whom I apprenticed for a year, I've never looked back! As an Authorized Practitioner of Infinite Banking Concepts, I now have the honor—and responsibility—of truly being of service and helping individuals, families, business owners, and entrepreneurs achieve financial peace of mind.

Life also is great on the personal front. My wife and I are so grateful that our wealth is safe, growing, and unaffected by the stock market, the government, big banks, and Wall Street—none of which have our best interests in mind.

My mission is to share this approach to wealth building with as many people as one man possibly can. I want to help people move from fear and uncertainty with their finances to confidence, control, and clarity.

Karyn Marie Kokeny

Karyn Marie Kokeny is a Certified 10X Elite Coach and Speaker. As a former Fortune 100 executive, Karyn led teams that consistently added millions to the company's bottom line. Since 2014, Karyn has been coaching business owners to multiply their income through marketing effectiveness and building high performing sales teams.

Karynkokenycoaching.com

ROLLER-COASTER RIDE FROM ADVERSITY TO TRIUMPH

Karyn Marie Kokeny

As I sit looking out my big picture window at the frozen lake, the following questions pop into my mind:

- What are your dreams and possibilities?
- Are you going after what excites you and brings you joy?
- What do you need right now to create your best business? Your best life?

I believe that with the right knowledge and mindset anything is possible.

I believe that the most important investment you can make is in yourself.

I believe that when you make a full, inspired commitment to your vision, nothing can stop you because you are powerful beyond measure!

I'm really blessed. I took responsibility for my health and got it back. I have an abundant life that includes a Caribbean oceanfront condo that provides me with one of my sources of passive income. My businesses are growing, and I get heartfelt rewards from helping business owners be their best selves, make more money, and get their life back.

But it wasn't always this way.

I grew up in the suburbs of Detroit, a first-generation American and the oldest of five. In the fourth grade, I discovered a balance beam in the school gym, launching my successful young career as a competitive gymnast. Committed, I practiced five nights per week and competed on weekends. Eventually my interest in boys and social life averted my attention. However, the incredible discipline I acquired from those years serves me well to this day.

Daily commitment and consistent practice to master your craft creates success.

The most distinct and poignant "thing" that shaped my youthful false reality and would damage my spirit is the tumultuous relationship I had with my mom. However, my dad was my rock, my mentor, and my compass.

It was February 1990. I was feeling on top of the world; I was newly married, had a strong six-figure Fortune 100 company job in New York, traveled throughout North America, stayed at hunting and fishing lodges, and flew on corporate jets.

On a business trip back to Michigan, my coworker Cathy and I had the opportunity to enjoy a dinner out with my parents on a Thursday night. My grandma (my dad's mom) wasn't well, so I stayed an extra day to visit with her.

Early Saturday morning, my dad drove me to the airport. I was worried about him; he was a medical doctor, and yet he was so unhealthy.

As chivalrous as my dad was, he didn't even get out of the car to help me with my luggage! That was SO NOT my dad!

He said he would wait for me until he knew I had gotten to my gate.

My strong gut instinct told me something wasn't right, *yet initially I didn't give it the proper attention*. But once I got to my gate, I did an about-face and raced back to where Dad had dropped me off, but he had already driven away.

Back home in Connecticut that afternoon, I went into complete shock and utter horror when the call came from our parents' neighbor.

My dad, only fifty-nine years old, had had a massive heart attack and died.

I felt like my life was over.

That gut instinct at the airport I didn't trust enough to "do something" with led to heavy guilt I carried with me for years.

How could my dad be so unhealthy and die so young?

And how would I navigate through life without my dad? When Dad was alive, I was unconsciously aware he was someone I could rely on if I fell down or failed. Now my life raft was no longer here.

No one is going to save you. Your success is your own responsibility.

I made some decisions. I avoided all conscious emotions because it hurt too much. Instead, I became laser-focused on my professional life. Overachieving in my career, my life spiraled down, and within two years my beautiful marriage ended.

Several years later I was presented on stage with the prestigious President's Award at a North American leadership meeting in front of hundreds of leaders and peers. It felt so surreal, invigorating, and exciting!

One thing is for certain: I didn't get here alone. I learned how to lead a team aligned with and rallied around a clear vision and mission. We operated on a set of values with clear targets, roles, and responsibilities.

I created strategies for the business, found a best-practice model of success, studied, and emulated it. I dressed professionally every day. I was continuously learning and growing while I "played the part," performing and delivering results. I was diligent in looking at the numbers to proactively steer the business. At any moment I knew the score, whether we were winning or losing, and we took the time to enjoy our victories along the way.

Had I run an eight-figure business before?

No. But I embodied **being** both a leader and coach, scary as it was sometimes, and as a result added seven figures to our bottom line.

With a highly demanding work schedule, I simultaneously trained for and ran full marathons in Alaska, Michigan, and Paris. Commitment to the goal, the training schedule, my coaches, and my determination got me across the finish lines.

BE your future you in every way and you will act accordingly and create what you want.

Meanwhile, I had been studying, observing, and talking with wealthy people, and I learned about investing for passive income. After a few "research" trips, I took massive action and put down a deposit to purchase a Caribbean oceanfront condominium.

Study success. Surround yourself with the right people.

My pipe dream was about to become a reality!

Yet something had gone missing. There was a crack in my foundation. Over the next ten years my life spiraled down again.

Finally, in 2012, I hit my lowest of lows. Our property managers absconded with $70K from my Caribbean investment—that money lost forever.

On top of that, I was in a job I hated, and I had just gotten divorced again, resulting in losing a lot more money. To make matters worse, I was faced with health issues and an upcoming surgery.

Then, on my first day returning to work after being on medical leave for twelve weeks, I was told that my job had been eliminated!

Alone again, my whole world was continuing to crumble.

Defeated, I was lying on the floor in my upstairs bedroom in total despair. I cried until I was at the point of complete surrender.

That was my pivotal, waking-up moment.

A long, long silence ensued.

Gradually I began to feel a spark, which evolved into a powerful spiritual connection. My words cannot do justice to the energetic strength I felt.

That experience provided me the two profound and final missing pieces to a life I now love!

1. I remembered that I am a child of God. I found my faith again.
2. I accepted 100 percent responsibility for everything that had happened and will happen in my life. Everything.

This allowed me to look at my role in everything and **know** that I'm not a victim.

This one realization has bettered my life the most.

Since 2012 . . .

- I've built a successful six-figure business as an entrepreneur.

- My businesses are growing. I'm continuing to invest in myself and my growth.
- I have five sources of income, including two passive income sources.
- My mindset is one of abundance and wealth.
- My relationship with my mom, now ninety-one years old, is the best it's ever been.
- I take full responsibility for everything in my life, and I'm creating the life of my dreams.
- I always have coaches and mentors to help me to stay accountable to my goals and dreams and to reach them more quickly.
- My vision pulls me forward, motivating me to take inspired action every single day.

Looking back, the actions that made me successful were so simple. I've done my best to highlight some of those actions here. Yet, it clearly has not been an easy road. In fact, I've traveled an incredibly long and winding road, a roller coaster of adversity. Unfortunately, some lessons had to be repeated. Ugh. But I NEVER gave up. That is the key to success.

There IS a shortcut to success. Learn from those who have gone before you. Invest in yourself with a mentor who can put up a mirror to your blind spots so you can avoid making similar mistakes and achieve your results faster and without pain.

If you think I can help, I'd love to hear from you.

Janet Krebs

Janet Krebs is a thirty-plus-year educator turned passionate parenting strategist. She has influenced the lives of more than six thousand students, fostering confidence, self-reliance, and self-esteem Today Janet helps families restore fun and intention in confident parenting. If you ask her, she will say she is living her dream.

www.janetkrebs.com

THE MAKING OF A MOTHER

Janet Krebs

I babysat one time in the early 1970s. The highlight of the evening was not the children but the novelty of eating a TV dinner. Somehow, I don't think the meal was supposed to be my takeaway from the experience. Clearly, I was not maternal.

Later, in an early marriage, I still did not see myself as a mother. I was enjoying California life as a DINK: double income, no kids. I was a student; I made money, made fun, made love, and was making a life. We skied, hiked, traveled—we were living the high life. There was no time or inclination to be tied down with a baby.

Nosy, well-meaning people chanted, "Don't wait until you're ready . . . because you'll never be ready."

One morning I woke up, and I was ready!

Benjamin Lee was named on the way home from the very first ultrasound, named after my father, Benson, who had died when I was eighteen. After an easy pregnancy and spectator-worthy delivery (translation: too enviable to share with most first-time mothers), the nurse handed Ben to me.

One look at him, and I knew what it would look like for Yoda to marry Mother Teresa and make a little bundle of joy ... resembling a shar-pei puppy. The nurses cooed, "Isn't he beautiful," to which I replied, "WHAT? This is NOT a beautiful baby!"

Right out of the gate, I did not win Mother of the Year. The nurses thought it was a terrible thing to say. I stand by the fact that I didn't say I didn't love him; I simply said he wasn't a beautiful baby. He WOULD be a beautiful baby in a few months when he grew into his skin, but not right now!

I was a tentative mom at first, not knowing what to do with this seven-pound human. But soon I relaxed and gave in to the rhythm of the new baby. Benjamin filled in his skin and became the Pampers poster child at three months old. He was such a pleasant child, happy and curious about everything.

By eleven months he was walking and talking, and this working mom was TIRED. One Friday night I showed Benjamin that I had put milk in a small Tupperware container on the bottom door of our side-by-side refrigerator. I explained it was for his morning cereal. With a toothless grin he acknowledged it, smiled, and off to bed he went.

Before I turned in, I left a bowl of cereal and spoon on the kitchen table where his booster chair was parked. I drew a heart on a napkin, which I used to cover the bowl.

The next morning, I woke up to a house that was eerily quiet except for the low murmur of voices. I held my breath as I made my way to the kitchen, where I found Ben sitting at the table, eating his cereal and watching TV with a grin on his face that stretched from ear to ear. My baby had assembled his own breakfast! And I got to sleep in—win-win! This mother thing was getting fun and exciting. This was one for the "things to repeat" list.

Baby number two was an even easier pregnancy and a three-push delivery. My makeup remained perfect as I didn't even break a sweat. The delivery room celebration was lingering and palpable until someone quietly whisked my baby boy away.

Within a few short hours, I was holding my perfect, beautiful son in his final moments of life. His lungs could not support life, and there was nothing the doctors could do save him.

Jordan Joseph lived for five hours and died in my arms.

In the middle of the night that February, I left the hospital with an empty car seat, empty arms, and a shattered heart.

How could this happen? Why did this happen? I never even considered that this could happen!

The pain was numbing and unbearable at the same time. This burden of grief became a uniform I wore every day.

It was cumbersome, and it got in the way of everything: my role as a mother, wife, and teacher. It made me blind to who I was as a woman. The weight of grief became a ball and chain that was too much to carry. I was unsure of my ability to carry on. Ben would find me crying and force me to be available to him. He saved my life by making me stay in the game.

It took the doctors too many months to give us answers. They were adamantly discouraging when I brought up trying again.

"We need more information; your autoimmune disease might flair up and be life-altering for the long haul; you must stay healthy for Ben."

Was Ben my miracle baby? Was I only going to be blessed with one child? Was there something wrong with me or my genetics? Since I had been adopted, I was in the dark with no medical history.

My stoic strength was developed in childhood. Defiant strength was the scar I used as a defense. This discouraging advice from "the experts" fueled within me a determination that made me deaf to all the naysaying. I ignored the critics and got pregnant . . . and miscarried . . . got pregnant . . . and miscarried. I wanted to be a mother again more than ANYTHING at that time in my life.

My fifth pregnancy was treated as high-risk. I was monitored once a month with a high-resolution ultrasound. My own thoughts gave way to terror and doubt on a regular basis. Pregnancy can cause mental trickery, and my tenuous history meant plenty of dramatic storytelling. I had G-D on speed dial, so when labor began, so did the prayers. On August 14, 1996, Elisa Grace was delivered as easily as the others. I think I had held my breath throughout the entire pregnancy and finally exhaled when we both cried together.

How does an experience like this shape a woman? What kind of mother would I become?

Broken yet resilient.

Strong on the inside and soft on the outside and knowing when it needs to be the other way around.

How profound was the struggle to create this family?

Did I become an overprotective, fearful mother? I had every reason to be one after all I had been through! Fear, insecurity, doubt, and trauma were all alive and well, running in the background like the ticker tape for the stock market. Could I do this—and what would it look like?

My two kids were a gift that I would never take for granted. I knew all too well the truth behind "the miracle of life."

Now that I had them, my job of developing them as humans was top of mind all the time. It shaped the kind of parent I became.

I soon discovered a magical balance between making my kids feel safe and loved while at the same time loosening the leash to allow them to grow and become who G-D wanted them to be. THIS was my mission, my responsibility, and the blessing of being a parent. These little people were counting on me to love them, shape them, and grow them to be amazing adults who would one day leave me and be amazing in life!

This was the kind of parent I was designed to be. It had been so easy to create that first instance for Ben to experience accomplishment and confidence when he made his own breakfast. It was too easy to find hidden opportunity to experience competence. Learning to do so many cool things that brought him delight and confidence brought me delight and confidence as well.

Elisa, of course, wanted to do everything Ben could do. It was so much fun observing them and allowing them to grow together.

Being a mom to Ben and Elisa made me a better teacher too. Over my thirty years as an educator, I had the privilege of touching more than six thousand students. The classroom foundation was so similar to home: warmth balanced with boundaries.

I knew and accepted my responsibility very early, and it shaped my approach to working with students of all ages, as well as with my own kids as they moved through the years.

I knew I was growing children to stand on their own. I knew they needed communication skills so they would always find their voice.

I knew they needed:

- grit and resiliency, kindness and generosity
- strength of body and mind, vulnerability and empathy

- to develop into problem solvers so they could always find their way
- to know their value and identity and not be afraid of being alone with themselves

Ben and Elisa are thirty and twenty-six respectively. They have long left the proverbial nest. Their wings are strong, and their hearts even stronger. Watch them fly!

Cat LaCohie

Cat LaCohie, LA-based British actress, speaker, and award-winning burlesque performer, "Vixen DeVille." Her unique training is designed for bodies of ALL ages, abilities, shapes, and sizes to break free of others' restrictive and damaging labels and instead rediscover and celebrate their inner badass, their inner goddess, their inner Vixen!

www.catlacohie.com

LIVING LIFE FOR YOU

Cat LaCohie

I was SO EXCITED! I was set! I was ready! In November 2004, I had everything in place. I'd just graduated with a BA in Theatre Creation as an actor in London... LONDON! Since age ten, I knew exactly what I wanted in life. I wanted to be an actor—and London was where it's at. Already off to a great start, I was living in an apartment with other creatives, right in the center of the action. I'd formed my own theater company with other performers I'd graduated with. I was even performing in an off-West End play where I was actually BEING PAID.

And then I met a guy.

He was a few years older than me, and I'd been dating a bunch of "college boys," so I was feeling ready for a "grown-up" relationship. With him being older, I chose to look to him to see what a "grown-up" relationship entailed.

What it seemed to entail was him questioning, criticizing, and subtly changing every single ... aspect ... of ... my ... life.

Have you ever experienced that? You start a new relationship, or a business relationship, and you begin to make compromises and change your behavior to make it work. Hearing phrases like:

"If you really cared about the company, you would..."

"If you really wanted this job, you would..."

"If you loved me... you would..."

That last one was the phrase that always got me.

Within three months of dating this man, that phrase got me to:

- leave the apartment I loved
- leave the friends that I loved
- get rid of possessions that I loved

Because, if I loved HIM...

It even made me consider giving up performing altogether when he, quite logically, said, "How long are you going to waste giving this 'acting thing' a go when you could just give it up now and get a proper job?"

It got into my head. I ALLOWED it to get into my head!

I had no confidence in myself, my ability, or my own thoughts and feelings to even *consider* questioning him. I willingly went along with it and submissively let it happen.

I wasn't choosing my life anymore; I was choosing his.

In less than six months, I had reshaped my life out of all recognition, and hadn't even realized it until...

A group of us traveled for a weekend out of town. It was a group (I began to realize) made up of *his* friends, *his* sister—even *his* ex-girlfriend. I felt like an outsider. We went to a music event, and as I looked around the room of around eighty people all chilling out and having fun, I realized I was not one of them. I was pretending to be what I THOUGHT they wanted me to be . . . and hoping to God I wouldn't be found out. I've never felt more alone. Every fiber of my being was screaming at me to leave—and I realized I couldn't.

I had completely allowed myself to relinquish all my independence. I had let this guy make all the plans, arrange the travel, the accommodations; it hadn't even occurred to me to ask for the information. This was before smartphones, before easy access to the internet, GPS maps, Uber. I couldn't call a cab because I didn't know what venue I was at. And it never even occurred to me to ask!

I couldn't leave . . . so I hid—I went to the bathroom and broke down. I stared at myself in the mirror and thought, *This is my life now—doing things I don't like, with people I don't like, pretending to be someone . . . I don't like—AND THERE'S NO WAY OUT!*

In the same way that I felt trapped at this event, I decided I was trapped in this life. And I'd done it to myself! I'd given up my freedom; I'd sentenced MYSELF to this existence.

My thoughts spiraled:

I hate this . . .

There's no way out . . .

So this is my life . . .

I hate my life . . .

But there's no way out . . .

So . . . THIS is my life. . . .

So.

I resigned myself to this being my life.

No sense in fighting it. I'd play nicely.

Months passed, and my ability to "play nicely" was tested. In complete contrast to my lifelong love of London, HE hated it; he said he wanted a "sense of freedom." His great idea? He decided we should buy a houseboat (but still moor it in the center of London!). I didn't quite know how much of a sense of freedom that would achieve, but if I loved him . . .

Before we'd met, I'd had dreams of buying ACTUAL property, having an investment in something that would give me stability, a home base . . . a home office!

But did I speak up? Voice my concerns? Nope.

I remained silent.

So now I'm going to buy a houseboat (that I don't want), and my meager life savings wasn't enough. But HE saw a way out! He suggested I call my family members—even the ones I didn't speak to—to see if they would lend me some money.

Did I speak up? Voice my concerns? Nope.

I remained silent.

I had the family conversations. I looked over the paperwork and realized I was going to be trapped in so much debt just so HE could have his sense of freedom. I became physically sick. I couldn't eat; I thought something was actually wrong with me. I didn't realize it was my body saying, "RUN FOR THE HILLS!"

When it finally came time to sign on the dotted line, I wondered if he really understood what he was asking of me. For me, my savings were my financial freedom to pursue acting. This commitment really would mean giving up on my dream. I really WOULD have to get that full-time "proper job."

BUT . . . I was willing to give that up for him, for us, if HE was 100 percent willing to commit to ME and our future together. Isn't that what grown-up couples do?

We were walking through our local park and started talking about pulling the trigger on the boat purchase.

I took a deep breath . . . I told him what this commitment meant to me, and then I asked him, "How committed are you? Am I the one you see yourself with? Are you 100 percent committed to us building a future together?"

He paused!

Then he nonchalantly turned to me and said, "Well, I don't think you're my soulmate."

My heart stopped.

He continued, "I don't believe in marriage. We'll probably have a couple kids, see how that goes, but I think you'll just cheat on me with some model/actor-type, and we'll break up."

WHAM!

I started processing what he was saying. So . . . he's asking me to invest EVERYTHING I have (AND DON'T HAVE) in a future that he doesn't even think exists?

Like a chess player figuring out their next eight moves, I started running scenarios of how my response would determine my fate. Could I FINALLY say, "I deserve more," and walk away? Where would I go? What would I do?

Then, the reality of what he'd just said hit me. I'd been willing to make all these sacrifices, for this person who was *everything* to me, and it meant nothing to him. *I* meant nothing to him.

And if I was willing to go to all these lengths for someone who thinks I'm THAT unimportant . . . *what's to stop me from being willing to do this for **myself**?*

I had been so willing to invest in HIS sense of freedom that it never occurred to me I could invest in my own! Right there, I decided to make that commitment to myself and MY life. I spoke up; we broke up. I said, "I deserve more," and walked away.

Once you commit to yourself—once YOU decide that YOU are important rather than waiting for confirmation from others, great things happen. I decided to go for what I REALLY wanted: my own place, my own stability, my independence (and yes, a home office!). I trawled the internet looking at apartments for sale and found that the money I was willing to scrape together and give up for the boat was just enough for a down payment. Three months later I bought my flat—and my freedom—and I vowed never again to let someone else's demands dictate my life!

I gained the confidence to know who I am, what I want, and then GO GET IT! I continued acting in London—until one day I realized that London was no longer enough. Once again, I said, "I deserve more," and began the long visa application process in order to move to Los Angeles. My commitment to myself fueled me against obstacles and naysayers until I finally packed up my life and got on that plane.

The day I moved to Los Angeles, by myself, for myself, I woke up to the sound of applause. OH! It was the LA Marathon crowd cheering on those running past my window! But I decided it was LA applauding me for grabbing life by the balls! I looked in the mirror and saw my soulmate.

My thoughts spiraled:

This is amazing . . .

THIS is my life . . .

There's ALWAYS a way . . .

This is my life . . . and I love it . . .

This is MY life.

Deanna Litz

Deanna Litz, founder of Powerful Nature Coaching & Consulting Inc., is a serial entrepreneur and multi-certified coach helping trailblazers develop the five essential skills for change-making across industry, scope, or scale. These skills form the backbone of high performance, confident leadership, and a life of health, wealth, and love.

www.powerfulnature.com

IT TOOK ONLY THREE WORDS

Deanna Litz

"There are years that ask questions, and years that answer."
—Zora Neale Hurston

We were finally in a good place with our marriage, our finances, our careers, and then the phone rang.

"Deanna? Is your husband there?"

It was Mickey, a neighbor from back home. What on earth did he want with Rick?

"Yes, Mickey, but what do you need him for? I'm right here."

"Just put him on."

"I'M RIGHT HERE, what's going on?"

"Your dad's dead."

And just like that, all my What Ifs turned into What Nows.

It took only three little words to shatter my world. The shock was completely different than that of my mom's yearlong battle with cancer almost a decade earlier. Love, grief, legacy, tradition, identity, and sanctuary all collided, and my entire relationship with the world changed. A complete loneliness and vulnerability set in, realizing that I was it. With great-grandparents, grandparents, and parents all gone, there is no buffer.

I started tackling the almost endless decisions of handling Dad's affairs, dismantling his livelihood, and dealing with generations of stuff. Then there was the big one—what was going to happen to the farm? It wasn't just the place I grew up, in my family's care for generations, on Treaty 6 Territory and the Homeland of the Métis. My connection to the land is in my bones and soul. It was where Nature became my third parent, my first love, and my greatest teacher.

There was a calling, and with it the biggest decision of my life—tougher than choosing my husband, my career, or passing on that lower-back tattoo. Now I had to decide: Would I step up and be the next generation to take the reins?

I didn't know what it would look like. Whatever it was, I *knew* we didn't have the time, energy, money, or resources to take on something this big this quickly. More terrifying was knowing that I couldn't do it on my own. I would have to have "the talk" with my husband. He had dedicated two years of our lives to serving in Afghanistan, and then two more years coming back to civilian life and rebuilding our marriage. Just weeks before, we had become mortgage-free. He was tired. What in the world was he going to say?

Sitting on the front steps, screwing up the courage to throw a monkey wrench into my husband's life, I watched neighbors walk by. They looked so carefree; they had no idea the world was about to stop spinning. I couldn't put it off any longer. I turned to my husband and, for the first time ever, spoke out loud the calling I felt in my heart to take over the family farm. I held my breath and waited.

For the second time in as many years, it took only three words to change my life forever.

"Whatever it takes," he said as he put his arm around me.

This was the turning point of my life, and the mantra that would rebuild it. My husband and I rearranged our lives. Friends called us bat guano crazy. We bought the farm and started settling into the unsettling truth that beginnings start with endings.

The cleanup began, including the old orchard—not a lonely job with all the memories of helping Mom and Dad plant it decades ago. They had even "let me" haul the manure. More recently we'd helped Dad find it again among the overgrown lilacs and maples.

Growing up, I wasn't sure what I wanted to be. A veterinarian was high on the list, until I found out it involved sick and injured animals. I only knew what I didn't want to be: a farmer. The stress, the work, the roller coaster of gambling with your livelihood to feed a society that just expects to be fed . . . getting stereotyped as dumb, ill-bred, uneducated.

And now I am a farmer.

Out of that orchard grew our idea to put in a garden. Then, to invest in some grow tunnels (three-season hoop houses) and begin market gardening.

Did we have market garden experience, or *any* real experience gardening?

No.

Did we thoroughly research the market first?

Also no.

We had a need to be of service. We had incredible resources in our hands and under our feet. We had some skills. What do you do with the gifts you've been given? We decided to follow our gut and put them to use. The vision and the resources took shape after we answered the call.

The first market garden crops were good. We made rookie mistakes, though, by taking a small-gardening mindset into large-market gardening. I asked every farmer I could, "When did you start feeling like you had a real handle on this farming thing?"

"I'll let you know when it happens," each one said as they chuckled.

The challenges kept coming. Early frosts. Irrigation issues. Crafty fox and birds and deer stealing our harvests, strutting around with their bright eyes and sleek, shiny coats from all that fresh, *beyond* organic produce.

And it turned out that my husband's tour "outside the wire" in Afghanistan was hardly an adequate training ground for farming with your spouse. *Was it worth it? Do we want to keep doing this? Could we even continue on?*

Life has a way of listening to our questions and giving us opportunities to answer them.

When the "Storm of the Century" rolled in and my husband was stuck in the city working his civilian and military careers to help pay for our farming habit, I hit the road to get to the farm ahead of the weather. It was up to me to save what we had been building. All that we had invested galvanized me, and it was now about *whatever it takes.*

The blizzard threatened to take down the grow tunnels, as they can't bear much weight. The winds caught the end of one and threatened to rip it apart. The entire end lifted out of the ground, sucking my heart up into my throat along with it. I jumped onto the tractor, moved it onto the tunnel supports, and raced on.

Every few hours around the clock, I bundled up, took a broom, and knocked off the snow all the way up the fourteen-foot centers, along both sides of the tunnels—the length of over two and a half football fields to clear. I'd go back inside to warm up under blankets with the hounds, since I couldn't get the furnace working. Then I'd head back out again, knock all the snow off, and head back in.

When the storm passed two days later, the farm was safe, and my husband was able to make it out, fix the furnace, and take the next shift. I had met that storm with an energy to match, and we came through.

Along the way, I've searched far and wide for things that would make this all easier. With a lot of trial and error, I would find a rare diamond to reduce the pain, help make me better, and let me enjoy the process. I started using what I found with clients, to great effect. I do what I do in my coaching and consulting business to save others from the headaches, heartaches, and backaches that aren't necessary but masquerade as inevitable.

My husband and I still work with Nature and the land.

I love having award-winning chefs on speed-dial.

I love hearing from parents how our fruits and veggies are gobbled up on the way home.

I love our relationship with the local soup kitchen.

I love the taste of fresh-picked raspberries still warm from the sun.

I love the wild bumblebees.

I love that our active military and veteran friends come out to help from time to time. Love taught me how the farm is a gift for them, too, and is part of my calling. I mean Jessie Love, a veteran. He loves that there are no distractions, no clock. He loves the healthy sunshine and sweat. Honest work. Real danger, as opposed to office safety cheerleaders who enforce rules about walking around with a hot cup of coffee.

I don't know how long I have here, but I won't let that stop me. We have put in asparagus gardens that could last several decades. My peonies could last one hundred years. We enjoy the shade of the trees my grandparents planted, even as we plant more.

Our calling is a signal sent by those who need it.

We are built to handle the pressures that come with our calling, as long as we understand our own powerful nature. Fortunately, we are all far more powerful than we realize, and far greater than the problems of the world.

You can't plan a calling, but you can respond.

"Who will answer for tomorrow?"

—Charles Péguy

Michele McHenry

Michele McHenry, RN, MBA, CEO, weight loss expert, and bestselling author of *Your Amazing Itty-Bitty Aging Well Book*, is an award-winning business leader, Woman of Influence, dynamic speaker, and founding member of the John Maxwell Team. She inspires women to become happy, healthy, and feel like a hottie!

www.michelemchenry.com

WHY YOUR LOST WEIGHT KEEPS FINDING YOU

Michele McHenry

Have you ever had someone tell you that you are fat? I have, and I will never forget that day. Even though it was the summer of 1978 and I was fifteen years old, it still feels like it was yesterday.

My mouth was watering as I was getting ready to pour delicious maple syrup on top of a yummy waffle spread with peanut butter. Just then my brother walked past me and said, "Are you really going to eat that, Michele? You're getting fat." What? Did I really hear him say what I think he said? My heart stopped. I was devastated. I felt UGLY and FAT!

I immediately threw away that waffle, went on a crash diet, started exercising, and lost fifteen pounds in fifteen days. Not a strategy I recommend! My brother's comment is one of the reasons I became a registered nurse and why I am writing this chapter today.

And just like 99 percent of America that struggles with weight, I started yo-yo dieting. It was like being on a roller coaster. I tried every diet out there, spending most of the time on the yo-yo diet roller coaster. Every time I stopped dieting, I'd gain all the weight back—and then some.

Finally, tired of this pattern, I began to study the science behind weight loss. I learned what works, what doesn't work, and what's necessary to achieve permanent weight loss. I had taken my last dieting roller-coaster ride. Now, at sixty years old, I'm at my ideal weight. I fit into my skinny jeans, and I feel like I am thirty again. And I want that for you too.

I started my career as a registered nurse thirty-nine years ago. For the first fifteen years, I worked in ICU, spending most of that time taking care of open-heart patients immediately after surgery. But I became really frustrated when I saw that so many people literally could have prevented what they had just gone through.

I got to see the devastating effects of what happens when you don't take care of yourself, and it really resonated with me. The problem with society today is that we never, ever think it's going to happen to us. In my experience, when you're not living a healthy lifestyle and taking care of yourself, it's not a matter of *if*—it's a matter of *when*.

This hit close to home for me because while I was in nursing school, my father had to have open, heart surgery at age forty-nine. Thankfully he recovered, started living a healthy lifestyle, and lived to be eighty-one.

My cousin Joel wasn't so lucky. He suffered a massive stroke when he was just sixty years old, and he died. He had a lot of living left to do, but he didn't get to do that. He was overweight, diabetic, and had heart disease. He didn't do what he needed to do to create the healthy habits and lifestyle he needed to live, and then it was too late.

So, taking into account my nursing experience, my family experience, and my professional experience, I became very passionate about health and wellness. What I came to realize is the common denominator: In all these life events, there is one word that really sticks out—*obesity*. The vast majority of unhealthy people are overweight.

When you think about being obese and the serious health risks that come along with it—heart disease, diabetes, high blood pressure, cancer—the one common denominator is being overweight. As a society, we have created an outrageous obesity epidemic in our country. The United States is number-one in the world for obesity.

My turning point came when I learned that diets don't work! If they did, we'd all be thin. It's not about the diet. The truth is that 95 percent of diets fail. That's a key problem for weight loss. You can DO everything right. But if you haven't addressed the real reason—your WHY at the foundational level—it just doesn't matter how many right things you do; you won't lose the weight permanently.

I discovered there are three components to weight loss: physical (your habits), mental (your head), and emotional (your heart). If any one of these is missing, permanent weight loss is difficult, if not impossible.

When you focus on you—on your whole body, mind, and heart—you can achieve permanent weight loss, freedom, fitness . . . and fun! There is joy and freedom on the other side of weight loss.

Some of you reading this are all about the FUN! Others of you might be thinking, *I don't even know what fun is anymore.* Many of you are somewhere in between.

Losing weight starts with your mindset. All success is 90 percent mindset and only 10 percent tools. I've learned that it's not about willpower, self-control, or motivation; eating is the result of three processes: neurological, habitual, and hormonal. Each of us has three neurological processes going on at the same time, for instance: your reward center, your inhibitory control, and your love of immediate gratification.

The battle to lose weight is in your head! Your brain is hard at work keeping you right where you are—safe and stuck. You are in a constant battle—no wonder it's so hard to lose weight!

Current scientific estimates state that some 95 percent of your day is spent in your subconscious. The subconscious is what I call your bodyguard. It controls your:

- Habits and patterns
- Automatic body function
- Creativity
- Emotions
- Personality
- Belief and values
- Cognitive biases
- Long-term memory

You think you are in control, but your bodyguard is really running the show!

Next is your spirit (your heart). What is your why? What is your belief system? What is your belief about yourself? What stories, thoughts, or lies keep holding you back from achieving your goals and permanently reaching your ideal weight?

Did you know that your mind-body connection is real and everything you believe about yourself starts from within? Your brain is powerful, and what you tell it, it believes. Your beliefs control your entire body. Your mind is always eavesdropping on your self-talk, even if you aren't saying it out loud. Your beliefs and attitudes about yourself can positively or negatively affect how your body functions and vice versa.

Les Brown says, "It's hard to see the picture when you're in the frame." He's right. You can't see the whole picture when you're inside the frame. It is virtually impossible. It is virtually impossible to figure out what your real why is because there's so much you can't see. Your why is buried deep in your heart.

Begin each morning by looking in the mirror and reminding yourself who you are and whose you are. You are a child of the Living God, and He loves you more than you could ever know. You are enough. You are beautiful. You are of infinite worth.

Now it's time to focus on your body. It's time to create those healthy habits to create the freedom lifestyle you've always dreamed about. Most of us fall into two beliefs, two whys:

- I know what to do; I just don't do it (or I don't do it enough).
- I've tried everything, but nothing works, so it must be me.

Either way, you feel like you are broken. You feel hopeless and helpless. Trust me, though, there's nothing wrong with you!

Ask yourself, "What would life be like if I never had to worry about weight again?" How would life be different for you? What would you be able to do that you can't do now? What is it worth to you?

So, what is the secret to lasting weight loss? The secret is YOU! You are the ultimate secret weapon. It's all about healing your inner you, your bodyguard, who wants to keep you safe so you don't get hurt again. It's about taming the inner critic that wants to keep you stuck so you don't change—because your bodyguard's sole mission is to keep you alive, and change is scary to your bodyguard. But you can learn how to talk to your bodyguard so that inner critic feels safe enough to let you create your new freedom lifestyle!

It's about conquering your fears and finding your inner confidence so you can break through your limiting beliefs. It's about retraining your brain, being consistent, and creating healthy habits, so your bodyguard wants those instead of what you are currently doing.

If you want to look better, feel better, and perform better in every area of your life, I encourage you to start today and focus on your body, mind, and spirit so you can build the life you love and find the freedom, fun, and joy on the other side. Now is your time. Take action now so you get the results you've always wanted. You are worth it!

Tim Mitchell

Tim Mitchell is an internationally known content writing expert and book consultant. He has ghostwritten for more than 150 entrepreneurs, coaches, and speakers in five different countries, enabling nearly one hundred of them to become bestselling authors by leveraging their expertise. He helps clarify their marketing message so customers will listen, resulting in more clients and sales.

www.timmitchellwriting.com

WHAT IS IN YOUR HAND? FROM TIPPING POINT TO TURNING POINT

Tim Mitchell

When I was in my twenties, I met Joe, a guy a couple of years older than me, very intelligent yet down-to-earth, but also a bit eccentric in some ways. We quickly became good friends, and he, with his wife and son, would spend a considerable amount of time with my family over the course of several years.

One day, Joe randomly said to me, "What is in your hand?"

"Um, nothing," I replied. I had no clue what he was talking about.

After that, he would often ask me that question, and I was always confused by it. When I would ask him why he kept asking me the same question, he would merely respond with the same inquiry, "What is in your hand?"

After my usual response, I would uncomfortably change the subject, and the conversation would take a different direction. However, I would often think of that question even when Joe wasn't around. It's like he planted a seed inside me, and I found myself regularly rehearsing that question in my mind.

I moved away from the community where Joe lived, and over the course of time, our communication became less and less, until we completely lost touch with each other. I know we had talked about many things and had some very deep philosophical and theological conversations during our friendship, but the only discussion I can remember today is the haunting question he would frequently ask, "What is in your hand?"

I would later find that very question to be pivotal in my life.

Over the course of many years, I have been blessed to work in various positions of leadership with progressive levels of responsibility from full-time pastoral ministry and counseling, where I learned to listen and help others develop pathways to freedom, to a fifteen-year career in financial services where I acquired extensive knowledge in money management and important principles of business, to owning my own business, which is one of the best teachers in life.

However, after years of successful business experience, to my astonishment, doors that were once wide open began closing, leaving me without the income level I had grown to enjoy. It felt like my world was closing in on me, and I became filled with significant uncertainty about my future. It was unlike anything I had ever experienced.

One day as I was driving alone in my vehicle, I was in deep contemplation about my circumstances and feeling sorry for myself. Suddenly, I spoke out loud these words: "I am cursed!" Immediately recognizing those words and the thoughts that prompted them as self-sabotaging, I quickly began to remember all the good things I had experienced in the past and continued to experience. I forced myself to make that my focus because I knew if my mindset wasn't right, I would continue to sink.

Without a doubt, I was at a crossroad in my life where I needed to reinvent myself. I was at a distinct tipping point. Frustration was gnawing at me, and desperation was knocking at the door. It was like starting all over again. My entrepreneurial mind began whirling with ideas, but honestly, it was a confusing time. I needed to do something, but what?

Then I remembered the question, "What is in your hand?" I could almost hear Joe's voice as I rehearsed those words in my mind. This became a very contemplative and introspective season in my life.

In my hand was a rather broad spectrum of experiences. Based on my background, this led me to believe I could potentially be successful as a business consultant.

It was a great idea, but how would I even get a business to consider what I had to offer? After all, I was an unknown at that point. My pondering continued. How could I get my foot in the door? What could I do to begin developing the relationships I would need in order for others to trust me with intimate details about their business?

Then I remembered that something else was in my hand. Throughout my varied career, I had always written extensively. I had a gift of making ideas come alive on paper. I was one of those people in college, and especially in graduate school, who actually enjoyed drafting lengthy research papers.

That was it! That would be my "foot in the door"! I determined that to build a trust factor, I would begin by offering my services to write about local businesses as a way to create a community "buzz" and attract more customers for them. If I didn't charge for my writing services, surely they would jump at the opportunity.

I began contacting small business owners to let them know I wanted to help them spread the word about their business through written content to be locally published. My prediction was right! Every business I contacted said, "Yes!"

The fourth business owner who said yes was a local chiropractor. He was very appreciative of the work I did for him and forwarded my article on to an international branding agency with whom he was already working. I had no idea the chiropractor was already working with a firm to promote his brand.

On a Tuesday evening at 9:18 p.m., I received an email from the CEO of the branding agency (I still have the email). The message said in part, "I saw the article you wrote. . . . We handle a lot of PR work for clients like Dr. Mark, and I was wondering if you do freelance work.... Please let me know, and thanks."

That email started a writing career that has exploded into writing for more than 150 business owners and entrepreneurs in a variety of business verticals in five different countries. I have been the ghostwriter for nearly one hundred bestselling authors, have written masses of marketing copy for mid- to high-ticket businesses, as well as writing multiple six-figure grants for nonprofit organizations. That 9:18 p.m. email turned my tipping point into a turning point that catapulted me into writing opportunities I never dreamed I would see.

I eventually transitioned from writing for the branding agency to owning my own writing service, and I continue to write for some of the best people in business without spending a single dollar on advertising. Every writing opportunity I have received has been through referrals.

While contracting with the branding agency, one of the clients I worked with was an online marketer. As his ghostwriter, I was very pleased to see the book we worked on together move to bestselling status. Several years later, after I formed my own writing business, this person contacted me about another book he wanted to write. He explained that after becoming a bestselling author, his world changed dramatically, and a plethora of opportunities opened doors for him to network with some of the leading voices in the online marketing world. As a result, this individual became a thought leader in his field, and his business has been thriving ever since.

He credited much of his success to his book writing experience with me and was interested in partnering with me in a more formal way since many of his clients were interested in writing a book. To make a long story short, we joined forces and developed a very synergistic relationship, together creating a publishing company, a book writing coaching program, as well as several other initiatives. We have also been able to create programs that are uniquely transformative for business owners and make a significant impact in the lives of our clients.

We help our clients find and express their voice based on their gifts and abilities. One of the significant components of our program is helping business leaders write and publish their own book under one of our exclusive book categories.

This journey has been extraordinary! I often reflect back on that period of time when I felt defeated, drained, useless, and unwanted. Sometimes you have to reinvent yourself! One thing life has taught me through painful circumstances is that opportunities will find you when you begin moving toward them. Here are a few other lessons I learned that may resonate with you:

- Always be aware of what is "in your hand" (your strengths) and how you can use it.
- When you stall out in life, begin moving again, in some direction, utilizing your strengths.
- It is much easier to steer an object in motion; direction will present itself.
- Walk through the open doors to see where they lead you.
- Don't be surprised if you are steered in an unexpected direction—embrace it.

May your "tipping point," while likely painful, lead you to a "turning point"—resulting in a lifetime of success!

Marlon Mueller

Marlon Mueller is an investor, speaker, author, coach and ambassador with Servio Capital and Philanthroinvestors. His experiences include modeling, farming, real estate and syndication, banking with life insurance, and raising capital. He coaches people on strategies to become financially independent and how to provide generational wealth—mentally, financially, and spiritually.

www.marlonmueller.com

FROM FARM BOY TO MULTIMILLIONAIRE

Marlon Mueller

> "It is the blessing of the Lord that makes rich
> and He adds no sorrow to it."
> —Proverbs 10:22

I grew up as a fourth-generation farmer of two family livestock and cropping farms on my mother's side. My parents lived on one farm, where my grandmother grew up, and my grandparents lived on the other farm where my grandfather grew up, less than two miles away. Both farms were similar in that both great-grandfathers had their large Victorian homes built in the early 1900s, and both included large livestock barns.

My father was a hard worker and usually had one or two full-time hired workers. It was always full-speed ahead, and I learned to work hard too. My father also was not afraid of debt.

My grandfather was the opposite. Unlike my father, who was in his forties when I was a teenager, my grandfather was in his seventies and walked through life at a slower pace. He patiently showed me how to use tools, take care of trees, and taught me many life lessons.

I remember late afternoons sitting on the porch swing with my grandfather as he told me stories that became teaching moments for me. My grandfather lived through the Great Depression as a young adult, and this had a huge impact on the way he thought about money. He was always talking about how many farmers lost their farms during the Depression because of the debt they carried. His own family lost their second farm, which was almost paid for, because they could not make the bank note payments. He then went on to help his father for many years to keep the main home farm and erase their debt.

I left the farms to attend the state university, where I studied soils and crops.

Returning home, I changed our cropping operation to make it more efficient and profitable. We were doing well for the most part, but just like the physical storm that destroyed some of our barns, there can also be spiritual and economic storms.

It was during one of these economic storms, the farm crisis, when I learned first-hand how debt could control my life.

I remember it like it was yesterday. My father and I were on one side of the desk, and the loan officer was sitting on the other side of the desk. The loan officer said, "Well, boys, you are going to have to mortgage your land for us to renew your note."

I began analyzing that our debt had been more the previous year and they didn't need our land as additional security. With less debt today, why were they requiring our land? I asked him the only intelligent question I could think of: "Why?"

The loan officer's only answer was, "That's the way it has to be."

My father was ready to sign, but I stated: "We need to discuss this further." He agreed, and we left.

I went to some of my successful business friends who were much older and wiser than me and shared my situation with them. None of them thought that it would be a good idea to mortgage the land.

Have you ever been at a point when you have no money to continue your life?

That's where we were. We had to make some major changes, but eventually we came out stronger. I understood raising crops, but I didn't pay attention to the economy and how interest, tariffs, or other money decisions made by the government or the banks could control our farming operation and financial well-being.

That was the first major turning point for me to ask: "How does money work?"

My wisdom with money grew in church. The pastor was teaching on tithing and challenged us with Malachi 3:10—"'Bring the whole tithe into the storehouse, that there may be food in my house. Test me in this,' says the Lord Almighty, 'and see if I will not throw open the floodgates of heaven and pour out so much blessing that there will not be room enough to store it.'"

This quote is the only time in the Bible that God challenges us to test Him. Our pastor said that if you tithed to the church and a year later you didn't see a blessing, he would return the money.

With a no-risk challenge like that, I figured I had nothing to lose.

Interestingly, after nine months, even though I could have used that tithe money—I realized I did not have any unexpected repairs and healthcare expenses—I saw how I was being blessed financially.

I also studied some Christian ministries' teaching on biblically based financial wisdom. I learned that there were about seven hundred direct references to money in the Bible along with hundreds more indirect references. Nearly two-thirds of Jesus' parables deal with the use of money.

I learned a lot of the basics such as making, saving, and investing money. One of my mentors told me that making money was easy; keeping it was the hard part. I got really good at saving money on expenses—from insurance to buying vehicles and using credit efficiently.

But how do you learn how to invest in pre-internet days when you're living in a small rural Iowa community?

I tried learning from magazines like *Money*, attending local seminars that provided some education but really were selling products, and from financial salesmen who came to my home. The problem was that every salesman believes he has the best product, and I did not know how to discern what made a good investment.

One of my first investment mistakes was buying a decreasing term life insurance with an annuity. The annuity was paying 10 percent interest for the first year; this would grow, and the term life would eventually not be needed. That was great, except the next year the annuity went to 4 percent. This money was locked in with early penalty withdrawals. I could be getting 5 percent from a bank savings account! I learned quickly that I had bought the wrong product for someone in their twenties.

Unfortunately, I bought into many programs thinking they would create the wealth to become financially free. The problem also was that I didn't know for several years that the program(s) was not going to create the wealth I was seeking. **Not only did I lose money, but more importantly, I lost time.**

Eventually, through bad decisions I learned to make good decisions. I continued to study and read many books, learning about all types of insurances, entity structures, types of trust, and different investment vehicles. Just reading about these things, however, does not make you an expert.

For instance, I got into buying tax liens as they paid 24 percent interest in Iowa. That return was great, but I discovered that there are different scenarios and risks. For example, don't buy liens on mobile homes in the country as they may not be there, the property may be foreclosed by the bank, or there might be unknown environmental issues.

Fortunately, as my knowledge grew, so did my network of high-net worth people. As the saying goes, "Your network is your net worth." Today, I network with millionaires and billionaires in mastermind groups.

I've learned about different private equity investment deals that are safer with cashflow and tax breaks, without risking the ups and downs of the stock market and gambling my future years when I cannot work. I've learned to leverage money using debt wisely, increase my wealth, and make the same dollars work for me two and sometimes three times at the same time, just like banks do. But more importantly, I now understand the time value of money and what it represents.

As one of my mentors told me, if I have a problem, and it's a money problem, if I have the money, then I don't have a problem.

Imagine a life like that. Once you have enough money to meet your needs, your focus needs to turn toward others.

Pastor Jim Baker, founder of Wealth With God, says that most Christians say they just want enough money to meet their needs. But isn't that being selfish?

Poor people cannot help the poor. His definition of prosperity is that "you have more than enough resources to fulfill every divine assignment God has for you and enough left over to help others to fulfill theirs."

I've spent the last thirty-five years studying wealth principles. I've made many mistakes, but finally I became financially secure. I went from farm boy to multi-millionaire. Today, my assignment is sharing my wisdom and knowledge to help you create your legacy wealth.

I've discovered the right connections for mentorship, the right investment vehicles for leveraging, the right protection for wealth transfer into the third generation, and offset your greatest expense: taxes.

> "A good person leaves an inheritance for their children's children."
> —Proverbs 13:22

My legacy is to teach my family and others "the wealth whys" that I understand and the values that I have learned; that my legacy is not about how much money is passed on, but the impact for doing good.

Sara Murray

Sara Murray is the founder and CEO of Murraki Salon. Passionate about the prosperity of stylists working behind the chair, she is an educator and stylist coach and the creator of The Stylist Source, a business coaching program for salon professionals.

www.thestylistsource.com

LESSONS FROM A STRUGGLING, STARVING STYLIST

Sara Murray

Even when I was just six or seven years old, I loved the idea of styling people's hair and making them feel beautiful. I remember saying, "I want to be a hairstylist when I grow up," while my friends would say normal kid things like "I want to be a teacher" or "I want to be an astronaut."

When I enrolled in beauty school, I was so alive with excitement to learn that doing hair was even cooler than I had imagined. There was creativity, science, technical skills, and best of all, the chance to impact how people feel.

As a hairstylist, you are granted the unique opportunity to touch people, both in the literal sense and by connecting deeply with them. You have the unique opportunity to see into the windows of their life experience from appointment to appointment.

Hairstylists have long been compared to therapists because of their soft skills, such as listening and creating a safe place to unload the stresses of daily life. Stylists build long-lasting relationships with their guests and experience many milestones with them. We laugh together. We cry together. We are there for first dates, engagements, weddings, funerals, pregnancies, baby's first haircut, first day of school, last haircut before college, and sometimes the very last haircut.

By touching just one person, a hairstylist can create a positive ripple that extends to touch hundreds more. Hairstylists help people restore their self-confidence and feel heard.

I've learned that it's about so much more than just hair.

As I write this, I have been a full-time hairstylist for eighteen years, and I have experienced a lot of ups and downs in that time. In the beginning, even though hairstyling was my life's passion, I found myself as a struggling, starving stylist. My first years in the industry were really tough, and it was hard to make ends meet—and if I'm being honest, I have to admit that even at years seven and eight, I still couldn't pay my bills.

I did have some good days when, at the end of a long, hard day, I would leave with hundreds of dollars in my pockets. I would feel rich! Yet the very next morning, the bills would come in and all that cash would be completely gone. I had the experience of touching a lot of money but never getting to keep any of it.

My money situation got worse and worse. One day my phone rang. I looked down at it and stopped breathing. I swallowed hard and just put my phone back in my pocket. I could see the number and I knew it was a creditor. I knew my credit card was maxed out, the minimum was overdue, and I didn't have any money to pay it. I got a sick feeling in the pit of my stomach every time I saw a number I didn't recognize because I just knew it was a creditor calling.

I hated that my money was always spent before I got it. My utility bills were overdue, and I was scraping by on rent. I had learned the perfect balance of how late a person could be on a payment without getting the service shut off or completely destroying their credit. I was always juggling just enough funds to pay bills on the day I absolutely had to. The only bill I consistently paid on time was my phone bill. I needed my phone so my guests could call to book appointments, so I couldn't risk it getting turned off.

Is this what they meant by "the grind"? I was up for the grind when I thought I would sacrifice for a little while and eventually get a big payoff. However, by this point I'd lived like this for years and was just feeling ground down.

Everything started to get dull, and my passion began to fade. The world felt overwhelming to me, and I was stuck. I imagined life having so much more to offer, and I felt like I let myself down. I was broke, and life was passing me by. I'd criticize myself by saying, "I thought I would have been further along, and I should have accomplished more by now."

After years of being worn down, I had my turning point.

I was given the opportunity to attend a seminar. I was honestly skeptical about it, but I was also desperate for a change. People who had gone through the program claimed wild results, such as growing their business 300 percent in just one year, paying off all their debt, investing, traveling, and doing the things they always dreamed of.

I didn't have money to attend and couldn't afford the time away from work; however, I just knew I couldn't keep living this way. I was tired and ready to give up. I decided this was my chance to give it my all because I didn't have anything left to lose. If it worked, it would change my life for the better, and if it didn't, it was over anyway. I borrowed the money, made the time, and committed to doing whatever it took.

By the time I made it to the seminar, I was feeling at my lowest low. I was so broken and had so much anxiety that I could barely breathe. I had a tight feeling of dread in the pit of my stomach. Somehow, through my fog, I heard the words that would begin to change my life: "Success leaves clues."

The concepts and ideas I learned in that seminar were not brand-new. Most of them sounded like common sense, and yet I hadn't been applying any of them. No wonder my life looked the way it did.

I have gained so much since that first seminar. Now, reflecting on my experiences, here are the three main lessons that truly changed the trajectory of my life:

1. Find Connection.

First, find a mentor. The first thing I realized is that I didn't need to reinvent the wheel. I needed to find a mentor who had already achieved what I wanted. If I followed their modeling, I could do it too.

Next, find a community. I learned the principle "You are the average of the five people you spend the most time with." If I wanted to improve the quality of my life, I needed to improve the quality of the people with whom I shared my time. Instead of hanging with others who were broke and complaining, I needed to be around those who were successful.

I learned the importance of accountability and of making a really honest distinction between what you want and what you need. I found that oftentimes what I needed was not at all what I wanted, and what I wanted I didn't need. My community helped me stick to what was best for my future.

2. Follow a proven system.

Before having a system, I fell victim to making emotional decisions, from a disempowered place, that cost me tens of thousands of dollars.

I learned to borrow proven systems used by successful companies outside of the beauty industry, and I merged them with strategies that are necessary for success behind the chair. Having a system in place allowed me to make the best decisions for myself and my business and helped me grow the confidence I needed to earn my worth.

I discovered that when I followed a system and focused on the results, I didn't have to stress over what to do. I learned that repetitive daily actions have a large impact on the results we get. Building daily, intentional habits positioned me for success almost automatically because I was following a system to create my ultimate outcome.

3. Develop a mindset for success.

What really catapulted me forward was knowing what truly I wanted—and why. I needed to be really clear about where I wanted to go to have any chance of getting there. Having clarity and cohesion allowed me to build my road map.

From there, I cultivated and embraced a wealth mindset. I learned that there will always be enough; I learned to make my intentions known; and I learned that to show up imperfect is better than not showing up at all.

Once I formed habits from these principles, my life started to fall into place. The joy and passion returned, and I could breathe again.

I now get to live out a life that fulfills and empowers me as a salon owner, brand educator, and coach. I've made it my mission to make sure others don't spend years like I did feeling lost, burned out, and wanting to give up. I now have resources to help stylists go from struggling and starving to fulfilled and financially free.

For anyone reading this (especially any stylists), I want you to know that the world is full of opportunity, and we all deserve to live our passion.

Nanette Nuessle

Nanette Nuessle, MD, is a graduate of the University of Missouri School of Medicine and the founder of Beat Down Burnout, a premier healthcare coaching company. She has been interviewed on multiple podcasts, including *Fried, the Burnout Podcast* (the number-one burnout podcast in America) and *The Podcast by KevinMD*.

www.beatdownburnout.com

LET'S STOP THE BULLYING IN HEALTHCARE!

Nanette Nuessle, MD

I'm a locum pediatric hospitalist. That means I'm a traveling physician who takes care of newborn babies and children who are sick enough to be in the hospital. I've been doing this for more than ten years, and I'm quite good at it. I love the lifestyle of traveling, learning new cultures, meeting new people, and developing new teams. I've worked all over the United States. During my travels, I've been troubled by stories of bullying. I've heard and witnessed physicians bullying nurses and other physicians, nurses bullying other nurses, and administrators bullying everyone. I'd never heard of nurses bullying physicians until I landed a job in a remote area of the Southwest.

It was a new Labor and Delivery unit, with all new staff, many of them travelers like me. At first, it was great. There was a good sense of teamwork and camaraderie. However, over the next several months, the travelers moved on, and the permanent staff arrived. I found myself working with a charge nurse who took an instant disliking to me. She argued every order I wrote. She argued policies with me, including policies that I had helped write. Part of my job was to educate new parents and grandparents. Part of my joy is to educate new nurses. However, when I did either of these, she would follow behind me and contradict everything I said. It was frustrating and illogical, especially since I had more training and more experience than she did.

It caused a lot of stress and anxiety in our unit, and staff began transferring to other workspaces, such as Med Surg or ER. This is unusual. Labor and Delivery is a coveted workstation. People don't die there. New life is happening. It's normally a very happy place to work. Yet the dynamics between this charge nurse and me made it anything but happy. Staff wanted nothing to do with that; they wanted out. The charge nurse started throwing things: throwing my things into my call room or throwing paperwork at me. These things always occurred when there were no witnesses.

This caused a lot of stress for me. I began having frequent headaches, stomachaches, and diarrhea. I saw a specialist who tentatively diagnosed me with Crohn's disease, then later changed it to irritable bowel syndrome when testing for Crohn's was negative. I would become nauseous the night before my seven-day work shift. Then it was the entire day before work. Soon it was two days before a shift. I couldn't calm down, no matter how much meditation, yoga, or exercise I did. I began to question my abilities as a physician and whether I should continue in medicine.

I tried talking to Ms. Charge Nurse several times, but it did no good. She took these opportunities to openly mock me. Mind you, I have more than thirty years' experience in healthcare; she had five. I elevated this to my department head. The way she listened to me made it clear that my situation was unimportant to her; the department head wasn't the one being bullied. I tried talking to members of the medical executive committee. They didn't believe it was as bad as I described and recommended that I try talking to the charge nurse again. Every time I did, though, the bullying got worse. I finally wrote her up in an email to the chair of the department. The email was shared with my bully, and things escalated even further. Ms. Charge Nurse began withholding critical patient information.

When it became obvious that the charge nurse's behavior was putting patients in danger, I knew that something had to be done! I discussed this with one of my friends, and she challenged me. My friend pointed out that much of this was nothing more than a personality conflict. I was offended. I denied it. I was insistent that I was a victim of bullying.

Wait, what? Me, a *victim*? I'd never had a victim mindset. Yet there I was, buried neck-deep in self-pity. Was I going to allow one person to take away my power and self-confidence? No! So, my friend invited me to a mastermind on personality types. This led to me signing up to become a coach. Three weeks later, I learned that Ms. Charge Nurse and I had opposite personality types. I valued freedom and flexibility first, backed up by science and logic. She valued systems, structure, credentials, and rules. She specifically valued her interpretation of the rules, not just the rules as written or the spirit of the rules.

I began speaking to Ms. Charge Nurse using the values of her personality, and miraculous things happened. First, she didn't know how to respond. She couldn't start an argument with me or nitpick what I was doing. Secondly, her minions saw through what she was doing and stopped supporting her. Third, within three days, the anxiety level in our unit dropped from 10/10 to 3/10, and staff stopped leaving our unit. In three days, I shut down the unit bully.

As time went on, additional changes happened. Nurse managers from other units began asking me to teach conflict resolution on their units. Physicians asked me to help them negotiate contract renewals. Within two months, I was doing lunch-and-learn meetings with the staff. This led to increased cooperation both within and across teams throughout the hospital. I began working with other healthcare workers. I assisted a respiratory therapist who was struggling with similar conflicts, and she became head of her department. I helped a janitor become a case manager.

Next, I took on bigger projects at the organizational level. I worked with a large clinic where two physicians refused to speak to each other. When they saw each other in the hallway, they would each turn and go the other way. When they shared patients, it was up to their secretaries and nurses to gather past medical history, family history, and medication information. The clinic was unable to keep staff, who felt this was unsafe, quoting moral injury and concerns they'd lose their licenses. I brought in a team of coaches for a two-day retreat. Within half a day, we had those two physicians talking to each other, sharing stories and jokes, and catching up on old times. The week following our training, they worked together to revamp communication between their two departments. Now, shared patients get a physician-to-physician phone consultation followed by a summary note in the chart. When I followed up six months later, they'd lost no more staff, and their risk management numbers were greatly improved.

Learning to listen for and speak to a person's values not only transformed and bully-proofed my life, but it can transform yours as well. I'm seeking healthcare workers who are ready for an opportunity to learn a system that can drive bullying and burnout out of medicine, out of healthcare, and allow us to put the joy back into our professions. Will you join me?

Dr. Mort Orman

Dr. Mort Orman, MD, is an internal medicine physician and a leading anger and stress elimination expert. The author of twenty-three books on eliminating anger and stress without traditional symptom management techniques, he has conducted hundreds of workshops for doctors, lawyers, nurses, business owners, corporate executives, the clergy, and even the FBI.

www.truthaboutstress.com

HOW DOING SOMETHING I THOUGHT I COULD NEVER DO CHANGED MY LIFE FOREVER

Dr. Mort Orman, MD

"It's kind of fun to do the impossible."

—Walt Disney

Have you ever done something big or accomplished something amazing that you were "absolutely certain" you would never, ever, not-in-a-million-years, be able to do?

I've had several such accomplishments in my life—all of which surprised me greatly because I strongly believed they would never, ever be possible for me.

For instance, I didn't like reading or writing during my formal education years. Yet as of today, I have written twenty-three books, thousands of blog posts, and have read thousands of wonderful books, both for pleasure and learning.

Growing up, I never dreamed of becoming a doctor. In fact, I was sure this occupation was not for me. I hated going to see our family doctor, feared needles, and didn't like being around sick people, medical offices, or hospitals. Yet here I am today, retired from a long and successful fifty-year internal medicine career.

I used to be angry all the time and tremendously anxious about public speaking. I concluded many years ago that I would always be this way and it was "impossible" for this to change. Yet I've had very little anger or other types of stress in my life during the past forty years, and I have totally cured myself of all my public-speaking fears.

Also, based on my previous history of multiple failed relationships with women, I was pretty sure I would never get married (or if I did, stay married) and never have children. I could not have predicted this then, but my wife, Christina, and I recently celebrated our thirty-eighth wedding anniversary, and we have a wonderful daughter who lives thirty minutes away from us on the east coast of Florida.

My point here is that whatever you currently believe is possible or not possible for you to achieve in life, you are probably capable of much more, even though you might not know it.

My Biggest Turning Point of All

You might be wondering how I was able to produce all these major turnarounds, which have changed and improved my entire life. Well, most of the big ones (related to anger, anxieties, relationships, and stress) all came from another major turning point, which I also believed I was incapable of doing—not in a million, billion years!

This turning point came when I completed my first full marathon, in December 1979 (at age thirty-one). Now, you may be thinking, *Big deal—tons of people train for and run marathons every single year.* Yes, that's true. But given my prior relationship to running, it was a gigantic, life-changing, mind-blowing accomplishment for me.

You see, I had always hated running. It was one of the most unpleasant, painful, and demoralizing activities I knew of. I thought people who ran long distances were clinically insane and belonged in mental hospitals. Really, those were my exact thoughts. So I was absolutely convinced that I COULD NEVER RUN A MARATHON—after all, why would I ever want to? I didn't even go to the gym.

But after I opened my medical practice and started experiencing much more anger and stress, I decided to invest in personal development work. I started attending workshops, reading books, and listening to popular speakers in the personal development field. As I did this, my views of the world and of human beings expanded, and I started to realize that things I once believed in very strongly might not actually be true.

One day, I decided to find out if everything I thought I knew and believed about running might not be true as well. I made the "insane" decision to run a marathon five months in the future, and I knew that if I was actually going to do this and not have it be torture, I would have to find out if I was making running painful—and if true, exactly how I was doing that.

To my shock and surprise, I actually did discover that I WAS MAKING RUNNING A HORRIBLE EXPERIENCE, and it wasn't running's fault! During the course of my five months of training, I discovered more than thirty specific ways I was unconsciously making running way more difficult and unpleasant than it needed to be. These were ways I automatically thought about running and automatically (habitually) had been conditioned to approach it. Each time I uncovered one of these previously invisible INTERNAL CAUSES, I was able to correct for it—and the running became easier and more enjoyable.

I went on to successfully complete my first full marathon, December 2, 1979, with a time of 3:48. I then trained for and ran four more marathons, including two Boston Marathons. I also went on to enjoyably run more than two thousand miles a year for the next twenty-five years. In other words, I had miraculously and permanently changed myself from a person who hated running into a person who loved running and thoroughly enjoyed doing it over and over again. Prior to this turning point, I would not have bet any amount of money that this was humanly possible for me. But it happened for me anyway, and that's what I want you to focus on. I accomplished something I firmly believed was impossible for me to do, simply by uncovering and dealing with **previously invisible internal causes.**

Once I completed this improbable turnaround with running, other benefits started following almost immediately. I noticed that many of the same thought patterns and behavior patterns I had identified during my marathon training were also causing problems, mischief, and stress in other areas of my life.

And now that I had the experience of successfully searching for and identifying invisible internal causes (entirely within me) and using this knowledge to propel myself forward and accomplish things I thought were impossible, I decided to apply this same basic approach to other problem areas that were frustrating me.

I figured out the internal causes of my anger and public-speaking anxiety, and I was able to make both of these nagging problems completely go away. I figured out the internal causes of my relationship failures with women. I figured out the internal causes of much of my stress at work as a physician. And I eventually figured out the internal causes of almost every other stress problem I had been struggling with unsuccessfully for years.

The fact that I was able to cure myself of anger and stress actually goes back to my discoveries of how to cure myself of hating running. It all boils down to knowing how to pinpoint and overcome **invisible internal causes.**

For the past forty years, I've been teaching people all over the world how to be happy and successful with little or no anger or stress. I know how to do this because I know how to help them see the internal causes they were previously blind to.

I am retired from my active medical career now, but I still haven't stopped being a doctor and a healer. In fact, I can do more now to keep people from getting sick than I was able to do as a practicing physician.

Here is my dream for you:

I want YOU to have a happy, stress-free, healthy, and productive life. I want you have little or no anger, anxiety, or other emotional distress in your life. I want you to wake up each day feeling totally refreshed after a good night's sleep and excited to start your day. I want you to have strong and satisfying relationships in all areas of your life. I want you to raise happy, healthy, successful kids. I want you to have fun and laugh a lot while being highly productive at work. In short, I want you to not get sick, not feel unhappy, not end up divorced, and not ruin or handicap the lives of your kids.

You can have all this if you just learn to identify the **internal causes** of any stressful problem or problems you might be experiencing. All of the things I eventually accomplished in my life that I mistakenly thought were not possible for me were "not possible" simply because I didn't know how to identify the internal causes and the internal conditioning that was holding me back.

It wasn't really true that any of them were actually impossible for me. That might have been the case for playing in the NFL or the NBA. But for the ones I actually accomplished, I only "believed" they were impossible because I didn't know any better.

Fortunately, by reading this chapter, you now know better, so stop putting up with anger and stress in your life. You too can make the "impossible" anger-free and stress-free life—*you never thought you would achieve in a million, billion years*—possible for you and for those you love and care about.

Krys Pappius

Krys Pappius, founder of Krys Pappius Coaching, is a retired police officer who is now a coach, speaker, and bestselling author. Krys is co-author of the Amazon bestseller *The Game Changer v2* and *The Art of Connection: 365 Days of Transformational Quotes by Entrepreneurs, Business Owners and Influencers.*

www.kryspappius.com

TAKE BACK YOUR LIFE: FROM GOAL-ORIENTED OVERACHIEVER TO PURPOSE-DRIVEN HIGH PERFORMER IN THREE SIMPLE STEPS

Krys Pappius

I am a *high performer*!

- My purpose is clear: to make people feel seen, heard, and valued and know that they matter and their life matters.
- My values and my purpose guide my decisions—I am confident and have no stress.
- I have a network of friends in which everyone is accepted and celebrated for who they are—no judgment there!
- I set healthy personal boundaries.
- Mental, physical, and spiritual self-care are my priorities.

But it wasn't always like that!

In the early 2000s, I had all the trappings of success:

- I had a steady, well-paying job.
- I had no debt.

- I owned my home and my car.
- I traveled.

However, what the world saw was just a mask.

The truth was that on the inside my soul was slowly dying.

I was a people pleaser who had no self-confidence; stress and overwhelm were my constant companions; I spent my time either reliving traumas of the past or worrying about the future, where I saw nothing but more of the same.

To overcome my lack of self-confidence I had become an *overachiever*. My personal value was based on my accomplishments. Yet no matter what I did, it never felt like it was enough—*I* was never enough. So, I kept pushing myself to do more ...

It all came to a head on December 26, 2003.

It's 5:00 a.m., and I am coming to the end of a night shift. I am tired. In just under two hours, I will be curled up in bed sleeping ...

Then the police radio alarm goes off. Dispatch broadcasts a crime in progress. I am suddenly wide awake, and together with the rest of the squad, I respond to the scene.

My task is to do area patrols looking for suspicious vehicles and people.

At 5:20 a.m., I advise dispatch that I have a suspicious vehicle in view and I will be checking the driver.

I turn on my lights and siren. The vehicle pulls over.

I pull in behind it.

As I exit my police vehicle, I make a mental note:

- I am in an isolated part of the city.
- There is minimal lighting.
- It is deathly quiet.

I walk toward the target.

Suddenly, there is a deafening squeal of tires, and the driver takes off.

I run back to my police car.

I begin multitasking: talking on the radio, putting on my seatbelt, closing my door, putting my car in drive, stepping on the gas . . .

I accelerate onto a bridge deck that, unbeknownst to me, is covered in black ice.

My vehicle spins out of control. It slides across the bridge deck, smashes against the far side, bounces off as it gains momentum, slides back to the other side of the bridge deck. . . . On and on it goes, my car ping-ponging from one side of the bridge deck to the other, gaining momentum every time it hits the concrete railing.

It's a violent event. I know I might not survive . . .

As my car careened down the bridge deck, my life flashed before my eyes. It was an aha moment; suddenly I saw it all so clearly: Life was a disappointment!

- I had forgotten my purpose, and I had lost my way.
- I was lonely and unfulfilled.
- I had abandoned so many dreams.
- I had said NO to so many opportunities.

And in that moment, I promised myself that if I survived, I would do whatever it took to find meaning and purpose again—to find joy in living.

Eventually my police car slid head-on into a concrete pillar. Finally, it stopped moving; finally, I could no longer hear the scream of crunching metal.

It took fifteen months for me to heal mentally and physically from my injuries, to be considered "fit for duty" again.

I clearly remember the day I returned to work . . . I walked into the locker room, and put on my uniform and all the tools I carry with me. I looked in the mirror . . . and my heart sank. The person looking back at me was the same person who had been tossed around in the crash.

Nothing had changed—yet in that instant something did change.

I reconnected with my resolve. It was time to make good on the promise I had made to myself to make real changes, to turn my life around.

At the time I believed that asking for help was a sign of weakness—that I had to do it all myself. The task seemed daunting.

I signed up for all the courses and workshops I could find. I read as many books as I could. And while I found a valuable nugget here and there, the truth was that these resources were mostly . . . *fluff*. While they all gave me permission to dream, not one of them told me *how* to turn dreams into reality.

It was only when I took a step back that I could see how those apparently random nuggets could come together in a process that could lead to change. It's a simple process, just three steps:

1. Create a detailed vision of the life you really want, a vision that includes both WHAT you want and WHY you want it. When you know both your

WHAT and your WHY, you have clarity around where to focus your limited resources of time, energy, and money. More importantly, you have an emotional connection to the vision that propels you forward when things get tough.

2. Identify all the beliefs that that tell you why you can't have what you want out of life and debunk them. Your beliefs are simply stories you have internalized about how the world works and your role in it. The vast majority of these stories were internalized before the age of five, and they live in your subconscious. Until you take the time to identify them and debunk them, you are allowing a five-year-old to decide how to live your life.

3. Take action. You can't get *anywhere* standing still. If you want to make changes in your life, you MUST take action. But not just any action—you have to create a roadmap to your destination that is broken down into the smallest steps possible. That way you can make changes *one small step at a time*, celebrate every tiny achievement, and easily track your progress.

When I implemented the process, I experienced some early success. For example, since 1980, I had dreamed of hiking to the summit of Mt. Kilimanjaro in Tanzania. The only reason I had not accomplished that dream by 2005 was that my gremlins kept whispering to me:

- *You could NEVER do that!*
- *Who do you think you are?*
- *You are not someone who flies halfway around the world to climb a mountain!*

The time had come to replace those beliefs with my truth:

- *I AM* a hiker.
- *I AM* an adventure seeker who can do *whatever* I set my mind to.
- *I AM* someone who travels halfway around the world to climb a mountain!

In the fall of 2006, I finally saw the world from the summit of Mt. Kilimanjaro! As I stood there, looking down on the plains below, I felt more alive and powerful than I had ever felt in my life. I saw life as an adventure. I saw the world in all its beauty, richness, and texture.

I knew there was no turning back.

Over the next few years, I dusted off more dreams:

- I visited the mountains of Rwanda to experience the wild mountain gorillas.
- I explored Western Mongolia, where I witnessed a total eclipse of the sun and then went on to visit the Gobi Desert.
- I trekked the Jomolhari Trail across the Himalayas of Bhutan, a distance of one hundred miles.

Small step by small step, I became a high-performer: purpose-driven, confident, fully engaged in life.

You see, the first time you say "yes" to yourself, the first time you embrace and celebrate your success, you start an upward spiral. Your confidence grows just a little, and you ask yourself, "What's next?" With every step you take, you move further and further out of you comfort zone, steadily learning and growing and moving closer and closer to your dream. So I ask you this:

- What do you want in life and why do you want it?
- What is YOUR Kilimanjaro?
- What is that ONE thing you can do for yourself to light the fire of your self-confidence, to propel you, slowly yet steadily, toward being a high performer living your dream life?

Change takes time; there are no magic pills. My transformation took years because I thought I had to do it myself. But with support and guidance, your journey will be much shorter.

Will you wait for a near-death experience to blow dust off your dreams—OR will you say YES and take a step TODAY?

Roslyn Rasberry

Roslyn Rasberry is an "Authentic Being" facilitator, spiritual mentor, coach, speaker, and workshop leader. Her work can help you awaken to your personal power and "Remember Who You Are"—activating a life of purpose that you love and helping to change the world just by *being* yourself.

www.roslynrasberry.com

KEEP YOUR LIGHT ON!

Roslyn Rasberry

It just takes one moment to change your life forever.

I stood alone on the school playground as recess was ending that early summer day in sixth grade, just a few weeks from the end of the school year. I wasn't alone, but I *felt* alone, confused by what I was seeing.

It was actually a beautiful day. A gentle breeze was blowing, but there was something in the air that I didn't understand. It was noticeable. Palpable. I could feel it.

For the last few weeks, I'd noticed a growing, perplexing pattern among my peers. Great kids, mostly, whom I'd grown up with for years were now behaving cruelly and bullying one another.

There seemed to be a lot more out-and-out fights, kids being teased, and meanness. I didn't even recognize some of them anymore. I witnessed some sweet-natured, full-of-life kids suddenly becoming more subdued. Others were just plain sullen, with body language that illustrated a shutting down. I also saw kids turn away classmates they were once friends with, either making fun of them or calling them names in front of other kids to get laughs. There were those who tried to make themselves smaller, shutting down and hiding, while others tried to make themselves larger, intimidating.

It all just made me very sad. It felt like I was watching something end.

Then, suddenly, like a lightning bolt, it came to me—an intuitive clarity I still remember to this day. I heard a voice inside my head say, "Oh, they're turning their lights off!" This was a life-changing epiphany. So many, by their behavior, were turning off their brilliant inner lights. At that moment, I swore to do my best, for the rest of my life, to try and keep mine on.

Next year it was on to junior high. There would be different rules, pressures, and expectations. There would also be harsher social consequences. The subtext was that we weren't kids anymore, and it was time to start acting like the adults we'd be expected to grow into. We were trying to figure out and prepare for our place in the world.

It struck me that what I witnessed happening that day was, arguably, one of the most powerful, most defining moments of our lives. In hindsight, I came to see that it was also universal. No matter a person's nationality, race, religion, or socioeconomic origin, we all come from families, communities, and cultures that shape us with distinct messages and parameters of who and how we are supposed to be. Perhaps it was the young man who longed to be a professional dancer but became a football player instead or the young woman who wanted to travel the world but became a doctor in order to carry on the family business. I wondered:

Is compromising our core truth a *required* rite of passage into adulthood?

We disconnected at that moment, and we turned away from core pieces of our innate beauty and luminous nature, so we could be embraced by the "nurture" of a society and world that not only didn't understand that light but were threatened by it.

"The Event," as I sometimes refer to it, was not only disturbing but also **traumatizing**. For someone highly sensitive like me, it was devastating. I was aware that I was aware. I know I'm not the only one. Perhaps this resonates with you, too.

I came into this world an intuitive, openhearted soul, feeling and caring about all the things around me. People, trees, flowers, the earth—and the wind! The wind wasn't just exhilarating—it whispered! I knew that everything had life, a force, a sacred power.

I say that I made the choice to keep my light on, yet really, my soul didn't know any other way.

The thing is, I believe we all come into this world loving, lighted, whole, gifted, and unique. Full of wonder and inner brilliance, with *unlimited* dreams and believing that nothing is impossible for us. Our relationship with this essential part of ourselves changed that day. A separation began and along with it, a disconnection from how we see life, others, and ourselves. In many ways, it also influenced the ways we are able to give and receive love.

We are set up to forget who we are.

This matters because we each have a personal contribution to make—both to heal and improve the world that no one else can. Martha Graham, the iconic modern dancer and choreographer, once said that if we block this energy:

> *"It will never exist through any other medium, and will be lost. The world will not have it. It is not your business to determine how good it is, not how it compares with other expression. It is your business to keep it yours clearly and directly, to keep the channel open."*

My own journey forward has been a process and has not been without its challenges. Yes, I've kept the commitment I made that day in the schoolyard to maintain my own truth despite the daily effort of having to navigate the energy-sucking pushback related to any one of my social identities. Especially as a self-titled African-American, lesbian, woman of deep and pervasive spiritual personage, who also just happens to be a second-generation PK (preacher's kid). My mother's father was a minister and so is my father. Talk about pressure!

I've been too much for some people and not enough for others. I didn't listen to the right music, something was wrong with how I spoke, or the way I held my body. Too assertive, too strong (for a woman), too different, too sensitive, too intense. Too naïve (because "everyone in business lies," as a former employer once scolded me after my refusal to lie to a client). That was the last straw. It was then that I determined that I needed to work for myself.

The decision to keep my light on meant just that. I would not only *keep* my light on—I determined that I would *use* my light. The activist poet Audre Lorde said:

> *"When I dare to be powerful, to use my strength in the service of my vision, then it becomes less and less important whether I am afraid."*

It has also been extremely important to me to model what I felt there was a profound absence of, which is another way of being in the world—one that is love-based with an entirely new definition of power. A definition like the one created by David Hawkins, which states:

> *"Power is always associated with that which supports the significance of Life itself."*

Over time, I could see the absolute connection between dynamics being played out on the global stage and the situations many of us were experiencing in our personal lives—fractured relationships, health issues, abuse of power, violence. And I wanted to do something about it. I decided that there needed to be a place, a platform for the deeper work that so many people were yearning and longing for.

So, my own inner light led me, over twenty-five years ago, to create a business and work in the transformation field called "Vital Change." The tagline was

"Dynamic Change Through the Vehicle of the Human Spirit." I started out with motivational speaking and created and presented workshops, staff development programs, and facilitated community and university dialogue groups. The latter led me to being named one of Syracuse University's "Women of Distinction for 2013."

Since then, I've placed my business under my own name, while continuing to be a spiritual mentor, coach, and an "Authentic Being" facilitator. I am passionate and hopeful about both the different world we can create and the lives of well-being and aliveness that are just waiting for each one of us to claim.

Through my work and just by being who I am, it's been my privilege to have opened many closed doors and closed minds. Whether it's been in front of a room leading a workshop or a conversation with a person while waiting online at the grocery store, what I offer is the same. It's holding space for magic, a return and connection to our authentic selves—to the power of worlds that reside within us.

The good news is that it *is* possible to bring forth your own gifted light, to be a loving presence in the world, just by tapping into the personal power of who you really are and who you really came here to be. When we tap into the immeasurable resources housed by our inner being, we open ourselves to unparalleled resources such as creativity, dynamic connection, inner wisdom and knowing, healing, self-leadership, and love-based insights to issues that were once only viewed as unsolvable problems.

Please never underestimate the potential impact that a smile or eye contact may have to convey to someone that they are valuable, visible, and worthy. If you remember nothing else, please remember this:

> "A star earns the right to shine the day it is born."
> —Matshona Dhliwayo

The same is true of you. Keep your light on!

Mary Jo Rennert

Mary Jo Rennert is living proof that it's never too late to find joy and fulfillment, even after life-shattering loss. An author, speaker, registered nurse, grief specialist, and certified life coach, she helps divorced Christian women heal the past, improve the present, and create a roadmap for the future.

www.maryjorennert.com

FROM BROKEN TO WHOLE

Mary Jo Rennert

This past year was amazing! I spoke at conferences, gave workshops, and hosted my own events. My book *You Are Still Beloved* received an award, and my second book is nearly ready to publish. I traveled with friends and family and already have tickets for upcoming trips.

My ninety-year-old mother is my best friend, and my brother and two sisters and I remain very close. I have two brilliant, caring, loving children, an amazing granddaughter, and a lovely daughter-in-law. I enjoy helping other authors write and publish their books, and my work in divorce ministry is gratifying.

Okay, that's the "Christmas letter" version of my life today. But it wasn't always like that.

At age twenty, I married my childhood sweetheart. Glen and I were surrounded by long-term marriages. Our parents and my grandparents were married for over sixty years. After forty-four years, I had little reason to suspect that my own marriage wouldn't follow the same path.

But one morning at work, I received a phone call from a woman who claimed to be having an affair with my husband. She poured out intimate details about him and our children and offered to send me pictures and videos, some taken at her house and some at mine.

When I asked her why she'd called me, she said she was mad because he was messing around with her best friend.

During our conversation, she offered to get him on a three-way call. I thought, *What have I got to lose?* so I hit the mute button. The voice I heard was definitely my husband's. I listened as she accused him of cheating with her best friend and others. He didn't deny it. I quietly hung up the phone.

My office door remained open the whole time, and life outside that door went on without skipping a beat.

Yet in that fifteen-minute phone call, my entire universe fell apart.

Where do you go from there?

I was dazed and in shock, and I needed a quiet place to sort this out. I ended up in the chapel of a local Catholic church, where I sat with my eyes closed, too numb to think or pray.

I felt as if I'd come to the bottom of a breath and could barely inhale again.

In the stillness, I pictured myself as a little child with God at my side. He took me by the right hand and began to lead me away. I looked over my shoulder at my husband and reached out my other hand to him. Then God said, "No, he can't come with us now. He'll come later, but not now."

Despite my distress, I had a sense of peace and assurance that God would take care of both me and my husband, regardless of our circumstances.

That night after dinner, I confronted Glen. He admitted they'd been involved sexually. He stared straight ahead while he spoke and didn't apologize. I waited for some sign of remorse, but he remained distant and emotionless. I wondered, *Who are you, and when did you get a lobotomy?*

I was so upset that I didn't sleep for the next thirty-seven hours.

But Glen slept that night and went to work on his rental houses the next morning.

That evening—after I'd spent, without a doubt, the worst and most humiliating day of my life being tested for every STD possible and pouring out my heart to my parish priest—Glen walked into the house, laughing at something he'd heard on the radio, and asked me if I knew a certain talk-show host.

At that moment, I realized he had no clue how devastating his betrayal was to me. He simply expected I'd get over it and life would go on as usual.

I wondered who this stranger was, this man whose emotions seemed to have switched off when I'd confronted him. I'd expected at least some sign of remorse, some explanation, some attempt to seek my forgiveness. But none came.

I couldn't put the pieces of our marriage back together alone.

My husband's betrayal after forty-four years of marriage devastated me, but it wasn't the first time I'd experienced that kind of grief. When I was thirty-one years old, I walked in on a phone conversation I was never meant to hear between Glen and another woman. When I asked him if my world was about to fall apart, he assured me that they were only friends. I wanted to believe him, but in my heart, I feared that what I'd heard was more than friendship. I felt as if my foundation had collapsed.

Why did I stay? Well, divorce never crossed my mind. I wanted so badly to believe him that I convinced myself that what he said was true. Somehow, I knew we'd work through this, and it seemed we had—our life together lasted thirty-three more years.

Looking back, I realize we didn't "work through" it, though. Glen ignored it and acted as if it hadn't happened, and I buried it.

I told no one. The shame was unbearable, and I didn't want our family and friends to think any less of Glen or me.

I learned that you can outwardly bury those emotions, but inside, that trauma is as fresh as when it happened.

You can go through your life acting as if there's nothing wrong. Traumas big and small pile up until eventually something breaks. That unhealed wound will show itself mentally and/or physically. If you ignore or bury it, unresolved grief and pain will be there for the rest of your life until you address it.

Because I didn't deal with my pain, I was miserable and depressed much of the time, irritable and impatient with my children. Life no longer seemed to hold any joy.

Rather than hide or minimize my grief, I should have sought professional help. Instead, I toughed it out for two years and cried every morning after Glen left for work.

Finally, one evening, as we rushed to leave for a camping trip, I screamed at my two little children and my husband, "We're not going tonight! Get out of my sight and go to bed!" All three of them scrambled and left me alone. I plopped down on the sofa with my head in my hands, feeling numb and wretched, unloving and unlovable. I wanted nothing more than to be swallowed up—to disappear and relieve myself and my family of such misery.

As I sat there, I became aware of a warm, loving Presence that surrounded me and saturated my entire being. I knew instinctively this Presence was God. I felt no condemnation, no need to measure up or perform, just gentle acceptance of me in my miserable condition. My tears flowed as I sat bathed in this love and forgiveness. I no longer felt connected to the multiple distractions and obligations that had pulled me in so many directions a short time before. I was conscious only of the overwhelming love that enveloped me.

As I sat there, I understood that God loves me unconditionally and without measure—and not only does God love *me* that way, He has that same love for every person He's ever created, without exception. God, who is Love, can't not love.

That truth remains at the core of my relationship with God and my understanding of who I am in God's sight. In the many years since that experience, I've been tempted to doubt God's love, to go back to thinking I must earn it, that I've got to try harder, that I'm not worthy. The truth is, we can't earn God's love. None of us is good enough, no matter how hard we try. None of us is worthy. God loves us—not *despite* the fact that we're human, but *because* of it.

It's that assurance that has carried me through my journey of healing.

Losing the marriage relationship that defined me for forty-four years made me dig deep to discover who I really am so I could rise above the pain, the grief, and the humiliation I experienced because of my divorce.

This is what I learned and what I want to share with you:

- Your true value lies outside of any human relationship, including your marriage.
- No matter how unworthy and miserable you might feel, no matter what you've done or failed to do, God still loves you.
- Not only that, but God loves every person that same way.

Before my divorce, I had no idea how many other people were trying to navigate this difficult journey. I had no idea how little support is available and how lonely that journey can be.

So, my "mess" became my message.

My mission is to help others know they can survive tragedy, reclaim their joy, and move forward with confidence, clear vision, and power to rebuild their lives—at any age—especially if they've been wounded by divorce.

Karen Rigamonti

Karen Rigamonti is a physician and an executive, life, and organizational coach. She has more than thirty years' experience raising a disabled child and helping individuals and families cope with the stress caused by healthcare issues. By stressing compassion, she helps organizations to create a healthier workplace and provide more effective care.

www.drkaren.org

HUMANITY WINS

Karen Rigamonti

Wouldn't it be nice to have a doctor you just click with—one you feel really listens to you?

Wouldn't it be nice to have a place where patients, families, and healthcare providers communicate with compassion, dignity, and respect?

Wouldn't it be nice to be part of an organization that knows caring experiences produce the best outcomes?

Thirty-seven years ago, my son, Luigi, was born severely premature when an obstetrician would not listen to me, resulting in an intracerebral hemorrhage. It caused blindness, autism, and severe intellectual delay. My life was changed forever. I became a permanent family caregiver and learned the necessary tools to advocate for his needs and others like him. This helped me to overcome many emotions as I navigated a life I had never planned for, and it eventually propelled me to acquire certifications in coaching and leadership training.

I began to help families of other disabled children coping with stress and challenges. I knew only too well how overwhelming it was for me as a physician. I could not even imagine how others could manage. My circumstances also prompted me to join nonprofit boards serving disability, healthcare, and education. Frequently I drew upon my medical, business, and public health trainings and life experiences. Hope propelled me forward to find new options, resources, and possibilities. Slowly I came to believe that facing the task of providing long-term care to a loved one does not need to be the end of anyone's dream.

Years later, my husband was asked to go to Saudi Arabia to administer a major healthcare organization. It was an agonizing decision for me whether to take our son or leave him in the US where he had support, leave my other children and friends, and resign from the nonprofit boards that aligned with my work. I finally agreed to join him, expecting to continue my work to improve healthcare and help patients and families.

After our arrival, I discovered that the organization did not support my activities. I felt unheard and unseen. I felt stuck, far from family, friends, and my community, isolated and helpless. I yelled at my husband, "It's all your fault! You are not supporting me—we agreed that with our last child in college, I would be able to work again." I thought our marriage might end.

After several miserable months and much reflection, I came to the realization that I faced three choices. I could remain silent and suffer the consequences of other people's decisions, I could decide to go home, or I could stop blaming and take charge and find a way to be heard. I chose the third option.

I knew that, like me, too often patients and families are not heard, resulting in situations causing sorrow. I offered a pilot workshop entitled, "How to Communicate with Difficult Patients and Difficult Families." The staff began to understand that "being difficult" was the result of being ignored. The workshop was a triumph. The staff suggested another workshop on communicating with "difficult colleagues." This second workshop was also enormously successful. The positive feedback convinced the CEO, and he convinced the board to approve training all full-time employees.

Today, many hospitals, pharmacies, clinics, and other healthcare organizations say that they believe in person-centered care, but that does not usually assure that such care is provided. Efforts to incorporate efficiency and focus on the budget do not necessarily make the most effective and personalized experiences. The fact is that employees, patients, and families continue to complain that no one really appreciates and values them. Administrative concerns always seem to prevail over compassionate humanized care.

Creating and maintaining healthy cultures in teams and organizations isn't easy. How can we transform a whole organizational system and culture with policies and procedures? How do we make people feel more included and valued? I believe it is critical to share this vision at all levels of an organization, from the CEO to the janitor, if we wish everyone to feel relevant and become more engaged and productive.

For this major organization to be certified as a person-centered healthcare organization, it was necessary to train 85 percent of the four thousand full-time employees in proper communication and collaborative work. I thought that we needed to do better. As a result, all full-time employees were required to take two interactive workshops on communication and compassion totaling several hours. For those in frontline positions, we added an additional two-hour workshop on how to interact with people with disabilities.

Next, I wanted to tailor a program for the one thousand contractors. Most of them were term workers from foreign countries. The duties of contractors were more menial than those of full-time staff and included landscaping, housekeeping, and food service. I was told that contractors did not need to be included in our workshops. I insisted that we train everybody. I combined a training on sensitivity toward those with disability with trainings on communication and compassion. It was an interactive abridged version of the training received by the full-time staff with different exercises relevant to contractors.

This was the first time these employees had been grouped together in the auditorium like staff. I mixed laundry workers with landscapers, kitchen staff, cleaning staff, and maintenance people. I gave examples from each of their disciplines of how they were important to the daily functioning of the hospital. I pointed out that a cardiac patient could die if the electroshock could not be provided due to a malfunctioning power outlet. I said, "The organization needs you to make sure the electricity is working. The hospital needs your cleaning, so no one gets infected. Cleaning a spill prevents someone from slipping and breaking a bone. People may not always recognize you, and for that I truly feel bad, but know that you are important people here. Without you, no one else can do their job well."

It was an epiphany for them. For the first time they felt appreciated and valued. The contractors understood that I respected them as partners. It was the first time anyone had thought to provide an interdisciplinary training for them. Through the interactive exercises, even though they could not all manage exercises perfectly or speak English fluently, they were not ridiculed, as I continuously showed them how hard and challenging the exercises are for anyone.

These contractors had always been at the bottom of the totem pole—"nobodies" in comparison to the rest of the staff. They had never felt seen and heard before and appreciated me sharing personal stories from my life and family with them. They told me how the things I talked about were the same values stated in the Koran and what Mohammed's teaching discusses. "Yes," I concurred, "all the great religions preach compassion and respect, especially for those who are in need of support such as those with disability."

And that's how it's done. We can honor people differently, but we should maintain similar standards at all levels of an organization, regardless of the individual's role. This is key if we want to really acknowledge and respect individuals as dignified human beings. Today many organizations are checking the boxes for diversity and inclusion, but unless their employees feel they belong and are equally valued, they are just putting Band-Aids on a problem rather than addressing it.

Contractors and full-time staff feeling like valuable assets are more likely to want to stay at the organization and work hard. During the five years that I spent in Saudi Arabia, the results were more dramatic than I imagined; employee engagement as well as patient and family satisfaction went up for each year I worked there.

I confirmed that compassion and gratitude are critical for the staff to feel good about themselves. The staff understood that is critical for the patients and families to feel heard for treatment plans to be successful. I was living my vision by changing the culture of the healthcare system. I learned that with compassion the world responds positively. Caring experiences of employees and patients/families generates quality results. Isn't that what we all want? To be seen, heard, and understood? To be appreciated, valued, and respected? To enable quality results? It does not matter what our background is, what our job title is, what our ability level is, we all want this.

We all are faced with difficult life circumstances. When we choose to have life's circumstances work for us, we can discover the gift or opportunity from all life's trials. We can recreate joy and purpose in our lives. We can move from chaos and uncertainty to confidence and happiness.

Now back in the US, I continue to support individuals and organizations. I explain why we can experience patients, family caregivers, nurses, doctors, or administrators as "difficult." They become difficult when they feel like we do not listen to what they are trying to communicate.

It is our birthright to be respected and heard. Actively listening and communicating with compassion in all interactions deepens our relationships, which then become more caring and trusting. When relationships are deeper, collaboration increases. More collaboration increases safety and improves outcomes. Better experiences and improved outcomes increase loyalty and that leads to a much better organizational performance.

Humanity wins.

Lynne Roe

Certified professional coach, business growth consultant, and change maker **Lynne Roe** helps entrepreneurs and small business owners develop a strong foundation of leadership so they are not the only ones who can run their business. She takes business owners from entrepreneurs to CEOs of successful, profitable businesses.

www.lsrconsultants.com

BUILD A BUSINESS TO SUPPORT YOUR LIFESTYLE

Lynne Roe

Owning a thriving and profitable business is exciting. Doing so and taking five weeks of vacation each year is exactly what I wanted for my life. It sure didn't start out that way, though ...

My daughter Cindy was my inspiration for creating the successful and flexible business I now have that is professionally fulfilling and profitable.

During her freshman year of college, Cindy called me. She had slipped on the cement stairs at school and landed on the back of her head.

Cindy was at the infirmary with a concussion. She was confused and had severe migraines. She asked if we could please bring her home for a couple of weeks while she recovered.

Of course, there were tests and doctors who all said she would recover in two weeks to two months. When she didn't recover right away, the doctors started saying two months to two years.

Meanwhile, Cindy needed assistance just to walk, or she would bump into walls or fall down. Mostly she was lying in bed and wasting away, literally. Her migraines were severe enough that she couldn't eat much. She was a tiny thing, only about 105 pounds when she was healthy, and she was losing weight fast.

The doctors were little help. They just said to give it time—only now they were saying two years to perhaps this being permanent. Cindy lost her personality too. She had been a fun person with a great laugh, but we hadn't heard that laugh for years.

It was a very dark, very scary time for us.

It was three years before we found a treatment that began to make a difference for Cindy. It was about eight years before her personality came back and we could see our daughter again. And after more than ten years, she finally went back to college full-time—as a twenty-eight-year-old freshman.

When Cindy fell down those stairs, I had just started my coach training and was excited about growing my business. But then I needed and wanted to stay home and care for Cindy. I also knew she might need that support for the rest of her life.

I realized that if I were to have a business at all, I needed a plan—one that would fulfill me professionally as well as my hopes and dreams of owning and running my own business again. And be flexible enough to care for Cindy. So, I set to work to design a business that was successful and still flexible. Of course, there were ups and downs and bumps in the road.

I focused on the wrong things at first. I was concentrating on my offerings, my packages, pricing, and what was included. That all seemed logical, but I didn't ask my prospective clients what they wanted. I knew what they needed, and I was right about that—but *they* didn't know what they needed. I eventually learned to combine what they wanted and what they needed for even greater success.

I didn't focus on building relationships in the beginning. I just thought, *If I build it, they will come.* Believe me, if they don't know you or your business, you won't have people banging down your door—you will have crickets.

I did set up some systems in the beginning, but I learned quickly that systems need to flex and adapt to changing environments. The one thing I did right in the beginning was to get help learning everything I needed to know to be successful. I worked on my skills as a CEO, even though I was the only employee in the beginning.

As each year passed, I got better at planning my business, became successful and profitable, and still had time to support Cindy. That's when I realized that I had created a Strategic Planning System that could adapt to most small businesses. I began helping other small business owners implement plans for the growth of their businesses using the same strategic planning system.

Owning your own business isn't easy. Most entrepreneurs start their business so they have more control over their income, their time, and how they serve their clients. Unfortunately, many end up making less money and working too many hours. They struggle because they didn't think through what they needed to build their business.

The fact is that owning your own business is a lot of work, so if you're not going to get what you want from the business, it is easier to work for someone else—no worries about making payroll or paying invoices, no concerns about accounts receivable, problems can go up the chain of command to someone else, etc.

But if you are going to own your own business and work hard to build that business, then build the business that allows you to live the life you really want.

- I believe that we should own our business; our business should not own us.

- I believe that our businesses should support the lifestyle we want to lead.
- I believe that our business will only grow if we grow. Each business owner must become the leader their business needs.

Did you know the average American spends about fifteen hours planning a one-week vacation? You have to plan where to go, how to get there, and what to take—and you have to plan special activities to make sure everybody is happy on the trip.

Most importantly, we have to plan for the time and the money to pay for that vacation. After all, isn't that why you decided to go into business—to afford special times like vacation?

But it's been my experience as a business coach that many business owners spend more time planning their vacation than they do planning for the success of their business. And guess what? Most small businesses fail in the first few years. So, let's get started planning for your business growth and make you one of the successful businesses.

To be successful, you need to set the direction for the business. What does the business need to look like to support the lifestyle you want to live? Set things up so the business runs smoothly. Then build your team so you're not the only one who can run the business. Give yourself time for a vacation, caring for a family member, or pursuing a hobby. Finally, plan so you will have consistent revenue and profit—why suffer owning a headache that loses money?

Three important things to remember about a plan for success:

- Start with the end in mind—what lifestyle do you want? Get really clear about this.
- What does the business need to look like to support that lifestyle?
- Make your plans to build that business.

Every business, regardless of size, needs a plan that encompasses all parts of the business: sales and marketing, operations, customer service, team development, and profit. Start to think like the CEO of your business. Ask what you (or your team) will need to be successful.

- What does the marketing/sales manager need?
    - Lead system—How do people become aware of you and your product or service?
    - Your marketing messaging—What problem do you solve for your client? How do you talk about it?
    - A tracking system—How will you ensure consistent sales?
- What does the operations manager need?
    - Systems and processes—How can others can pick up the job quickly and deliver the same great service?
- What does the customer service manager need?
    - Consider the customer experience—What do you want your customers to experience? How will you make that happen?
- What employee development do you need? (Build your plan so you are not the only person who can run the business.)
    - Who do you need on your team?
    - What skills do you need to hire for or train for?
    - What skills do you need to learn to become the CEO of the business you are building?
- What is your plan to ensure profit?
    - Does your pricing cover costs and ensure a profit?
    - How do you keep your expenses under control?
    - How will you retain that profit?

Your final plan is like a GPS for your business. You start with the destination: What is the business you want to build? Then you determine how to get there. Your plan needs to remain flexible, just as your travel plans are flexible. When something causes you to get off track, you find another path to the same destination. Growing a business never happens in a straight line; there are turns and roadblocks along the way. But if you stay focused on your destination, you will get there with perseverance.

You may not have a sick child, but I'm sure you have family and friends you want to spend more time with—or a hobby you want to pursue. Take the time to build a business that gives you the lifestyle you want by planning for it and constantly working in that direction.

Lamont Stephens

Lamont Stephens is a sought-after online marketing consultant who works with experts, coaches, authors, and speakers to create world-class coaching and consulting programs. His unique approach helps clients identify the missing puzzle pieces using his proprietary marketing and sales frameworks to create a lucrative online marketing business system.

www.lamontstephens.com

FUNDING YOUR DREAM

Lamont Stephens

Life was great! At least that's what I thought. I had plane tickets to Hawaii in hand. My wife and I had just moved into a beautiful new home and bought a new car. I had ambitious plans to build a family and create a life I never had growing up. One more semester was all I needed to finish college, and my business was going well. I saw what the freedom lifestyle looked like.

Then my mother received a call from her doctor just before our trip to Hawaii with the dreaded diagnosis: "You have breast cancer."

Questions raced through my mind. *What does this mean? What is going to happen to her?* Emotionally, I was shocked. To make matters worse, one week after this devastating news, my spouse informed me, with no explanation, that she no longer wanted to be married. Now I was doubly devasted and heartbroken.

My mind and emotions were so cluttered that I couldn't concentrate on finishing school, and my business had to be put on the back burner. Just as though someone flipped a switch, I found myself in a financial, relational, and emotional crisis.

After about a year, I came across an informational video promising I would make a ton of money creating "special interest" videos, known today as informational products. I began investing in more and more courses, products, programs, and software—all which yielded little results.

Obviously, these "gurus" lied to me! *They never tell you the WHOLE truth*, I thought.

I knew that I needed online marketing help. Unfortunately, I had to figure out on my own how to build a legitimate online business because I got tired of giving those greedy gurus my hard-earned money.

Honestly, I felt like a complete failure. I started to doubt myself, and I wondered if I had what it took to be successful. My confidence was way down. I was confused and frustrated and felt desperately incompetent.

After investing thousands of dollars, I started to prosper in my video production business, but there were tons of headaches that came along with working with people and shooting video.

In fact, my business eventually flatlined despite my best efforts. I was convinced that I could save my business if I invested in a coach to help me through this difficult time. I knew with great certainty after investing my $15,000, I would surely discover the secrets held only by the wealthy.

After all, I thought, *if I'm going to invest my money, I deserve a coach who will thoughtfully explain how things really work online.* I believed that people should be treated honestly, fairly, ethically, and with integrity. Dishonesty shouldn't be allowed to win or be rewarded.

While I learned a ton from the top industry experts—and in one group was even voted by my peers as "having the most impact on their business"—I sensed there was still something missing.

Some may call it ego or pride, but I am a competitive person. I refused to quit or be defeated. Someone had the answers I was looking for, and I was determined to find them.

Along this entrepreneur journey, I met some awesome guides who were making six and seven figures in their respective businesses. The information they shared was great, but again, it felt like there were pieces missing from the puzzle.

My side hustles made me enough money to continue on in my journey. One friend and leader, Rob Robson, shared a speech entitled, "Faith It Til You Make It." That was the journey I was on—a faith walk. I felt like God would place people in my path to help me along the way and encourage me to finish my course.

I wasn't just doing this for me. I was also representing all the people I envisioned I would impact as a result of fulfilling my purpose.

How long would I be walking in this wilderness? How long would I have to walk around this same mountain, listening to the same recycled information people were selling?

Suffering from "Truth Decay"

Truth Decay is a term I coined to describe online business opportunities that make BIG promises but never deliver on results. What a painful experience. Buyer Beware!

I know this from personal experience. Yes, I've been taken advantage of on more than one occasion by these individuals who are less than scrupulous.

Just when I was thinking about throwing in the towel, I met a master online marketing expert who shared secrets no one else had ever revealed to me. As I studied with him, he explained how online marketing worked. The epiphany from his mentorship was that I needed to understand the core steps that anyone who is launching anything online needs to follow. The difference between success and failure is getting the steps in the right order. As I started applying this to my business and clients, the results were amazing.

This was the turning point in my business. Once I realized that the gurus were just selling one step of the system without giving the context (the bigger picture), the game changed for me. I had been purchasing puzzle pieces from the gurus without understanding how the pieces fit together overall.

Finally, the mystery was solved, the secret revealed.

All the investments I had made up to this point finally made sense now. My team and I went to work, setting our systems, products, and programs to reflect this highly coveted industry secret.

When COVID-19 hit, my business continued to thrive. We were able to help other clients pivot, and our company was able to invest into other business opportunities and partnerships that would improve the lives of our clients and increase the value of our company.

On a personal level, my second wife really enjoyed remodeling our home. That's what I wanted for every one of my clients—the financial and time freedom to live life to the fullest.

One of my clients, Sandra, a single mom struggling to provide for herself and her son, was at an all-time low. She had everything within her to be successful, but she just needed a little validation and permission to step into her purpose. After giving her a plan, similar to the one my mentor gave me, she was able to leave her nine-to-five job and start a thriving, six-figure lash business.

I can't promise that you will receive the same results, but what I do know is that if you never invest in yourself, who will?

I decided I wasn't going to allow a previous bad experience to keep me from taking a chance on my future, and this led me to make another deposit into my dreams. I finally found an honest and open mentor who taught me the most critical skill set that I possess today: online marketing.

There are no words adequate enough to explain how it felt to have clarity and a success path that would get me closer to my goal. There was no longer any confusion about the customer's journey or mine.

Back to my personal story . . .

Life is great! I finally was able to make it to Hawaii and take a group of people with me. My mother, a cancer survivor, has been in remission for the past twenty-five years. Regarding relationships, I've found love again: three kids (adults now) and a beautiful granddaughter named Emily who adores her G-DAD.

Here are the lessons I've learned along the way:

1. Faith it til you make it. (Rob Robson)
2. Failure is not final; it's just feedback. (Simon T. Bailey)
3. Fund your dreams. (Lamont Stephens)

Patricia Stepler

Patricia Stepler is a high-performance mentor who utilizes an innovative, proven system for those who want to live the lifestyle they choose instead of allowing the world to dictate what they can accomplish. She is available to speak at your next event. Visit her website for a free audio.

https://www.patriciastepler.com/turning-point-gift-8099

WOULDN'T IT BE FUNNY

Patricia Stepler

My son, Danny, sat in the car, excited yet afraid, holding the large envelope with his scholarship letter inside. **"Wouldn't it be funny if this is a full scholarship?"** he looked at me and said.

For six years, if my son said it once, he said it hundreds of times: He was getting a full collegiate athletic scholarship. I was sure that, at age twelve, he did not understand how few athletes make it to the collegiate level. And by high school, I'm sure he started to realize that the odds were not in his favor.

Then, on top of that, he chose baseball. He had to know there were so few scholarships available for a team that rarely, if ever, was a full scholarship available. And yet he still believed *he* would be one to achieve such a feat.

Dreams like this just don't come true. For my entire adult life, I did personal development, set goals, and rarely if ever reached a moderate goal, let alone one of this magnitude. Yet after discouragements, plans that didn't work, and teams that did not select him, he still continued to believe the full scholarship could happen. What I didn't realize at the time is that success is not a secret—it is a science.

The mother in me wanted to protect him, so I was quick to remind him that the admissions office told us he could expect one-third to one-half the amount at most. After all, I didn't want him to feel disappointed.

Still holding the envelope, we reached our destination—a local diner. While sitting in the parking lot, Danny finally opened the envelope. As we saw the amount of his scholarship, our eyes grew big, and we both let out a scream. It was a full *academic* scholarship!

Immediately I knew he had caused this to happen, and yet I had no idea how. Sure, I was thrilled for him, but shortly I felt some anger. How could he accomplish this at such a young age with such little experience in goal setting?

I had tried so hard to achieve more in my life. I dreamed big. I wanted a life of abundance and a freedom lifestyle to do what I wanted when I wanted, never again to worry about finances. I wanted to be extraordinary. But here I was living a normal, average life, teaching school, raising three children, and living paycheck to paycheck.

For me, it seemed as though success was elusive, and yet sitting across from me at the diner was a prime example of what was possible. What did he know that I didn't? How did he achieve this feat? I knew I had to figure this out.

I began a search and discovered many "truths." I discovered ideas that prior to my son earning that scholarship, I would have found crazy. I found new mentors and coaches because I was so hungry for new information and awareness.

I discovered how strong my habitual thought patterns or paradigms were and how they were keeping me from moving forward. Unconsciously, success patterns were transferred to all three of my children as I shifted their paradigms through my personal development. I began to use this information as I taught my students so I was more effective in encouraging them to unleash their potential.

Wouldn't it be funny if I could have a similar success to my son?

My first transformation came as I followed these new success patterns and decided to go into corporate training. We're told that we become what we think about, so going into my classroom, I imagined that I was in a hotel conference room doing training for adults. Thoughts change actions, and soon I recorded a presentation that I sent to three different training companies. Since I was coming from the education world, I wanted to be better able to relate to businesspeople, as that was where I'd always wanted to be.

Before the end of the school year, the company at the top of my list invited me to work with them. I quickly retired from teaching children and moved into what I thought was my dream job. During the next eighteen months, I taught various soft skills, management skills, people skills, supervisory skills, and hiring skills to public as well as individual companies. In all, I conducted over one hundred full-day trainings.

As I continued to develop awareness, I increasingly became frustrated because of the agreement I had with this company. I knew the answers and materials the participants needed that would shift their habitual thought patterns. They needed the business I was developing, yet I could not tell them that.

Wouldn't it be funny if I could start my own business and help people to unlock their potential?

Through years of research and personal experience, I discovered that most people do not understand what they've done when they have success in their life and, therefore, cannot repeat it. I believe that three things must happen simultaneously for you to make a huge leap in success.

- **Think Bigger.** You are where you are because it is all you know. You must have a dream that inspires you to do the actions that are uncomfortable. Your dreams push you to plan, strive, and grow.

- **Become Bigger.** The person you are today is not the person you need to be to accomplish that *big* goal. Most of us struggle with confidence because we don't know who we are. You must be willing to push yourself and see yourself as having already achieved that goal. You can't give to others what you don't believe you are.

- **Play Bigger.** Playing safe is reality and won't get you to your goal. You must be willing to take a risk and do something different. Your plans need to be as big as your thinking. You must step outside of your comfort zone.

Learning how to think before you act is key, as your thoughts are what differentiates you from others. Gaining complete unwavering focus and determination that *you* are destined to succeed in your accomplishments and new actions will bring results as your mind fuels itself.

My journey to a new life was longer and more winding than I anticipated. Thinking bigger and playing bigger were no problem. However, my own paradigms and self-image kept me stuck and frustrated. Quitting was not an option. Determination and persistence were pushing me, as I deserved my desire. Focusing on my goal and seeing it in my mind's eye as already achieved became vital to my success.

Becoming more aware of what I wanted in life and living from the inside out instead of allowing the world to dictate to me, there now were times in my life when I followed the same pattern as my son to obtain goals for myself. I learned that awareness is the key to freedom in many areas of our lives.

Still not fully committed to myself because of the image I held, I often looked for the easy way or for someone who could help me. Once I was committed, however, the people, resources, ideas, and revenue began to come to me. My biggest missing piece was lead generation.

You can have the most wonderful programs, which I thought I did, and yet not be able to move them because you have no leads. Finding and learning the steps to effective lead generation became a game changer for me and one that I now help others to learn and grow their businesses.

This information has impacted my life in so many ways, and I am so grateful for this journey. Watching clients achieve their goals and build large businesses by shifting their mindset, hiring the right people, become great leaders, and find ways to do a process of lead generation is rewarding and motivating and brings me such joy.

Here are some thoughts I want to leave with you as you contemplate your next move.

Wouldn't it be funny if you could change your life by changing your actions and begin living the life of your dreams?

Wouldn't it be funny if you unlocked your potential and received more out of life?

You've got one life, so make sure to experience it to its fullest. You can do whatever you want. I am a perfect example of someone who was able to shift my thinking and self-image and become the person needed to accomplish my goals so I don't have to go to my grave wondering what could have been. That's my dream for you too.

The goals you are seeking are seeking you. Look at your results, and you will discover where your thinking is currently limited. You are the key to the most important person—you! You've been gifted with a purpose that you are meant to discover, and it lies inside of you. Go find it!

Jared Stull

Jared Stull, co-founder of the production company Stull Train Creative, is an award-winning actor, writer, and director. He and his wife, Nichole, coach businesses and entrepreneurs to connect with their audiences using storytelling frameworks and systems built on the principles of improv: Listening, Teamwork, Acceptance, Contribution.

www.yesandaction.com

ALL MY WORLD'S A STAGE

Jared Stull

Growing up, I was much like every other kid. I played sports, spent the majority of my time outside, built tree houses and forts, and generally had an adventure-filled childhood.

In 1986, when I was eleven, the movie *Top Gun* came out, and I finally knew my destiny. I wanted to be a fighter pilot. I wanted it so bad I could taste it.

I got to work figuring out what it would take for me to fly fighter jets. I checked out books at the library and learned about all the different fighters. I memorized top speeds, thrust, range, weight (both with fuel and without), armaments, and much more.

I lived close to a National Guard wing of F-16 fighters and would watch them fly for hours. To this day, the thunder of a fighter jet engine is music to my ears. It's the sound of freedom.

Both my dad, a veteran, and my grandpa, a former Air Force pilot, counseled me to embrace math and science so I could prepare to study engineering or physics in college. Most pilots have a deep STEM educational foundation. Not only that, both aeronautical engineering and astronautical engineering could have prepared me to be an astronaut.

Piloting a space shuttle? Yeah!

By eighth grade, I was on my way. I was athletic. I was smart. I loved math and science. I participated in bridge-building competitions and egg-drop challenges. I was in Boy Scouts. I knew if I got my Eagle Scout award, I had a better chance of getting an ROTC scholarship for college and a higher rank and pay grade when I got my officer's commission.

While finishing eighth grade, I enrolled in the bigger high school in the city and picked out my class schedule. I had general requirements and then had the option to pick two electives. I chose German as my first elective. I knew I needed two years of a foreign language to graduate, and I figured I'd get them out of the way as soon as I could.

My second elective was earth science. Kind of a repeat of my eighth grade science, but it would set me up so I could take chemistry by my junior year.

That summer at a Boy Scout leadership camp, I met a fellow Scout a few years older than me. He was going into his junior year and gave me some advice. He told me that French was a ton easier than German.

He also told me that the drama teacher let you swear in class.

We didn't swear in my house growing up, so the freedom to do it with the permission of a teacher seemed like a great idea. Plus, it was an easy A to help ease me into the new surroundings.

Well, that one choice—to switch from earth science to drama—completely changed my life.

The teacher, Mr. Bergquist, became the second most influential man in my life—the first being my dad, of course.

We could get extra credit by auditioning for the school plays. I got cast after my first audition in a play that was a collection of scenes written by students at a school in New Mexico. I was in two scenes, a super small part.

But there I met Julie. Julie was a sophomore, and she was gorgeous. Long, straight, dark brown hair, huge smile, and an infectious laugh—I was smitten. It just so happened that we played boyfriend and girlfriend in our little scene, and we got to kiss.

I wouldn't say that was the moment I stopped wanting to be an Air Force pilot, but it sure distracted me from that goal.

The next year I enrolled in the next level drama class and kept doing plays. I was cast as the lead in a play about a young high school boy whose imagination runs wild as he pictures his girlfriend making out with a jock football player.

It was a really fun script, and the cast was great.

This play wasn't one that we performed at our school, though. We prepared this play so we could perform it at the Montana Thespian Convention. That winter, more than six hundred high school theater kids from all over the state descended on Missoula at the University of Montana to take workshops, audition for colleges, submit for judging from the National Thespian Society, and perform these one-act plays for one another.

I had a blast! All these other kids were so interesting, so fun, so smart. I felt at home.

The resident stage manager coached all of the schools on how to get our sets onstage quickly and how to get our sets off as soon as we were done. There was a tight schedule because of the number of plays, and everything had to be done by the book. No time for curtain calls or bows.

Finally, our turn came. Nervously pacing, we watched the previous show from the wings. We hadn't performed this play all the way through in front of an audience. Would they like it? Would they hate it?

As a fifteen-year-old adolescent, I was going crazy. I didn't really want to get judged by a bunch of other kids. I wasn't super confident in my acting skills and had no idea how this would turn out.

Finally it was our turn. We stepped onstage. We set everything up, and we were off. I remember the first laugh we got. It was electric. A jolt of energy surged through me. Then we got a second laugh. And a third. Everything was clicking. Our timing was perfect. We had the audience rolling.

I remember thinking about three-quarters of the way through that I had the audience in the palm of my hand. It was such a specific thought and image. I could squeeze, and they would cry. I could tickle, and they would laugh. Whatever I did, they were right there with me. I was 100 percent connected to that audience.

We got to the end of the play, and everything had gone perfectly—everything. I delivered the last line, and the audience leapt to their feet . . . a standing ovation. It felt amazing.

But we didn't have time to enjoy it! We were on a time crunch and had to get our set off the stage within our time limit. We gathered our props and set pieces and rushed offstage right over to the stage manager. We dropped our things and started hugging one another and celebrating an amazing performance. It felt so good!

But that quickly changed. Over our celebrating and the applause from the audience, we heard that same stage manager yelling at us.

What happened? What had we done wrong? Were our things in the wrong place? Were we in the way of the next group?

Finally, he came up to us, grabbed me by the shoulders, and yelled, "You guys have to go back on! That's your curtain call!"

Six hundred high school and college theater kids, teachers, and professors were still on their feet cheering for us.

So, we walked back onstage and took a bow.

We were the only group to get a standing ovation. We were the only group that got to do a curtain call and bow after our performance.

It was amazing. In fact, it was life-changing.

Gone were the thoughts of the Air Force. Gone were the plans of being a pilot. Gone was the idea of studying engineering. I studied acting in college.

Halfway through school, I got practical and switched majors from acting to manufacturing engineering. I did Air Force ROTC for two years.

But I couldn't stay away from the stage.

Two things happened toward the end of college that changed my life for the better.

First, I started performing improv comedy. I got involved with a group on campus performing shows full of sketches and improv.

Standing onstage creating raw, unfiltered stories was the closest thing to the feeling I had on that stage in Missoula.

I realized that this feeling wasn't about being famous. It was about being intimately connected to an audience. Humans crave connection. All the theater

I had studied and the improv I was learning was helping me connect with people.

Second, about the same time, I met and started dating my future wife, Nichole. I don't think it's a coincidence that I was learning skills to help me connect with people at the same time I met a wonderful woman with whom I was able to connect.

Fortunately, she fell in love with theater and improv just as much as she fell in love with me.

For the past two decades, we've been connected. We coach on connection. We help businesses, entrepreneurs, artists, and creators connect with their audiences. We help families and couples connect with each other.

We want to hear your story and connect with you.

Nichole Stull

Nichole Stull, co-founder of the production company Stull Train Creative, is an award-winning actor, writer, director, and producer. She and her husband, Jared, are blessed to share their signature improv tools with their family and community, helping businesses and organizations forge stronger connections for the last twenty years.

www.yesandaction.com

FLIPPING THE "PROFIT" SWITCH

Nichole Stull

It was the biggest acting job we'd had to date. We were "Nichole and Jared" from the *ClickFunnels* video. It had only released a couple of weeks before, but the reaction was so big that ClickFunnels had paid us to attend their four-day conference in San Diego. So, not only did we have an online video that was getting thousands (and eventually tens of millions) of views, but now we were live and in-person at an event as guests of honor.

It was amazing! It was a dream come true! We had stars in our eyes. We sat in the VIP section with the speakers and the attendees who had paid a LOT of money to be there. We were literally rubbing shoulders with millionaires—business visionaries with whom we became friends. And everyone wanted pictures with *us*. They wanted to shake *our* hands. It was amazing!

And a little voice in the back of my head kept saying, *Who do you think you are? You're an actor. You're a fake. Your only businesses are failures.*

The voice was right. We had opened an improv comedy club and closed it within two years with thousands of dollars of debt. We had owned investment homes and lost them. We had dozens of business ideas and half-hatched plans. But ultimately, we were failures. We were barely scraping by, and while we had great love for each other and for our kids, love doesn't pay the bills.

That week was simultaneously really difficult—and also amazing!

I had the chance to be hypnotized by Marshall Sylver at the VIP kickoff night. I had decided that I was going to shut off every single bit of skepticism and just say "Yes!" So for the first time ever, hypnosis worked. I was 100 percent open. I remember every second of it. It was bizarre to be aware of the silliness and *watch* it happening from a place of zero decision-making because I had already given myself over with one choice to say "Yes!" It was freeing and exciting. And fun! I decided then and there to say "Yes!" with 100 percent conviction more often!

We had some of the most incredible conversations that week. We weren't total novices with the life and the lingo of entrepreneurs. All those failures had at least accounted for gained knowledge. And we had decided to learn everything we could while we were there. "Yes!"

But still . . . that little voice.

During one of the more technical presentations about the software program, I remember thinking, *I am an idiot. I thought I was smart, but none of that made any sense at all. What am I doing here?!* All the while, I was smiling for the camera and ad-libbing about every presentation and how great everything was and how it all applied to our life—ultimately, I suppose, proving how truly skilled I was at acting. It was imposter syndrome in a VERY real way.

So there I was, sitting in the front row listening to Marcus Lemonis speak. A real, live, genuine television star from the hit show *The Profit* speaking less than a dozen feet in front of me! His business was helping business owners, even struggling ones, succeed. He was talking about connection. He told these entrepreneurs, thousands of them, that they needed to connect. Not just connect, but that it needed to happen quickly and first. He told them it needed to happen in their elevator pitch! He explained that it isn't about what they do, but about who they are.

It was inspiring! My heart and head were in rapid fire.

Marcus had standing microphones in the two main aisles. He invited attendees to step up and try it out so he could coach them. Person after person stepped up and delivered pretty much the exact same elevator pitch they had always delivered. He would coach them a little. They didn't get it. In all of the little intros we heard, maybe just one implemented what Marcus was teaching. I was floored!

And then it hit me. He was telling them what was needed, but they didn't know how. If done for them (if he told them what to say), they could do it, but they couldn't seem to do it on their own. The only ones who were doing it on their own were the ones who were naturally good at it, and there seemed to be only a few of those. Everyone else struggled while I sat in my seat, flabbergasted. Because if I could have the microphone for just five minutes, I could tell them **how**. Okay, maybe it would take me fifteen minutes, but I could help 100 percent of the business owners in that room tell their story in the way that Marcus was imploring them to do.

Through my training as an actor and improviser, I had tools that could help these people connect quickly with their audience. And not just that—I understood **why**. As a storyteller, I could see both the **how** and the **why**, and as a coach, teacher, and director, I could help others see the **how** and the **why** too!

In that moment, I changed. I finally believed in myself in this arena. Not just as an actor pretending to be a business person, but as an actor who is a business person!

I had completed a certified life coaching course years earlier. I had been hired as an applied improv coach for businesses and leaders countless times. I had completed educational training courses and taught and presented for years. I had trained hundreds of people. But until that moment, I didn't understand the value I could give.

I had an entire life of skills that applied, but from where I had been sitting, all I could see were my "unqualifications."

What's more, I had this fire inside of me to help people, and I was letting it sit untended and dying out because I didn't believe in my value.

I had a new *thought*: What if I was being selfish by not helping people?

I left the conference with a newfound belief in what I had to offer and a renewed determination to make a difference. I knew I could help people connect to their audiences, their clients, and their families. I knew I could help them forge bonds through storytelling. I knew I could help them write their stories with simple tools and frameworks. I knew I could help them discover which stories to tell and get comfortable and real telling their stories in compelling, fun ways.

Then I let my doubt and fear of messing up slow me down. It had been almost six years since that moment and while I did help people, it wasn't on the scale I should. Every time someone reached out for help, I helped. I taught classes designed exactly as someone as asked.

But I was just waiting—waiting for someone else to tell me when my moment was here.

About a year ago, a college professor friend posted that he was bringing in people from the local film community, most of whom I would consider amateurs, to speak to his master of social work students on a variety of topics as guest speakers. I remember thinking, *What are **they** teaching?!* And then, with a little bit of indignation, *Why hasn't he asked me? I would be terrific at this!*

Another startling realization: How would he know that? Why didn't I reach out and tell him I could do it? Why didn't I ask for the opportunity?

So I did. I let him know I could come speak and offered a couple of topics that I felt I could really excel at for that audience. To my delight, he picked one and gave me the parameters. I poured my heart into it. I nailed it! He immediately asked me to return for future semesters!

It was an amazing experience, and not because I wanted to be a guest speaker for college kids. It was amazing because it was like a switch flipped again, for the third time …

The first was when I risked and said **"Yes!"** with 100 percent willingness, freeing myself to really experience and be open to the new.

The second was when I realized I absolutely have unique and important **value** to add and **contribute**.

And the third was when, sitting in my living room, I realized *I* must **offer** and take **action**.

It does me and the world no good to have a gift I don't share. And I can't just wait to share it until someone asks; most won't know to ask.

This last year has had the most projects and the most profit to date. That's not an accident! I have a new life motto—three words, one for each of these moments that incidentally combine my life as an improviser and as a filmmaker.

"Yes! And … ACTION!"

Molly Anne Summers

Molly Anne Summers is a Certified Professional Life Coach and has an advanced certification in energy healing. She specializes in relationships because every circumstance is a relationship. Her more than three thousand hours of life coaching and energy healing aid her in supporting those who want sustainable results for healthy relationships.

www.summersfordirectionandhealing.com

FROM BEING SUPPRESSED TO BEING EXPRESSED

Molly Anne Summers

To those on the outside, I had a perfect life. I was married to a career military man; I had two sons, and I was so proud of both of them. I worked as an executive secretary and was involved in women's organizations. I lived in a beautiful home in Wisconsin and had a master garden that was the envy of the neighborhood.

Within the walls of my home, I lived a much different life. My husband was physically and emotionally abusive. Being an abused military wife is very, very lonely. First, the police and the military are comrades. Had I called the police, it would have been his word against mine. Second, if I reported him, he perhaps would have lost his job and his future pension.

So, I told myself the story that staying with him was for the better. I didn't want to lose financial security and stability. I didn't know who would believe me anyway. Also, his job required him to travel a lot, so I thought I'd manage. What I wasn't paying attention to was how I was suppressing my voice in all matters.

My husband retired from the military in 2008. For the next year, he tried to adapt to civilian employment. That was a rough year. He was home a lot; he was angry and bitter. Eventually he was offered a civil service position in California, so we made the move.

It was during the move to California from Wisconsin that my life would change forever. My fourteen-year-old son and I were in my car following my husband, who was driving the moving truck. We were on a highway in Omaha, Nebraska. Suddenly, my car was hit from behind by an eighteen-wheeler, double-trailer truck! I had just managed to keep my car from spinning into oncoming traffic when I was hit a second time. The second time, the impact was so hard that my car flew into the air, rolled twice, and then flipped end to end, landing on its top. It flew so far up the embankment that it couldn't be seen from the highway.

As I was going through the air, yes, time did stand still. I was looking into my son's eyes. We were both wondering if the car would explode when it landed. I didn't see my life flashing before me. Instead, I thought of how I had wasted so much of my life worrying about things that may never happen. I realized that staying in a bad situation out of fear of the unknown was not even living. I remember clearly thinking at that moment that if my son and I survived, I would no longer live in fear. I would live full out. I would speak my voice. I vowed right then that living life to the fullest was the best example I could give my sons. Living full out was so much more important than financial security. I vowed to God that I would share these lessons.

Not only did my son and I survive, but neither of us had a scratch on us! The car was so totaled that it was not recognizable. An off-duty ambulance driver saw the accident and called us in DOA. When he arrived at the car window, he almost passed out when he saw that we were OK. I knew then and there that God had a mission for me.

I didn't forget my vow that day. Did the changes happen immediately? No. It took about a year before I filed for divorce. My ex became violent, this time with my son. That was the final straw. I called the police and had him removed from the home. Were my son and I financially OK? Well, not really. My ex-husband hid for a couple of months in order to not be served, so I had no income. Also, he moved 80 percent of his retirement income into disability so it couldn't be touched. (He had never served in a war; his disability was from elective surgeries.)

So, after I filed for divorce, I moved from the suburbs to the city, where I could find a job. My son and I came very close to living in my car for a month because I didn't have the necessary money for a deposit and the first month's rent. Fortunately, I found a job, and I took out one of those astronomical payday loans to get us into an apartment.

We went from a nice home in the suburbs to living in a one-bedroom apartment in the city. It wasn't the best area, but we were fine. No—we were more than fine; we were free! No more walking on eggshells. No more wondering what would trigger a rage. No more being afraid to speak.

One day I came across a group led by a life coach. I really wasn't clear on what a life coach was, but I met with her. That was another defining moment for me! I knew the moment I met her that the Universe had brought us together. It took me five years, but now I am a successful life coach working with people around "relationships."

Every Circumstance Is a Relationship.

Many of my clients are empty nesters. I have helped many of them to have solid relationships with their grown children. They now understand that by building their own lives as individuals, their children see that their parents respect the fact that they also have their own lives. I also work with parents and share tools to navigate raising young children. And I have helped many clients find their relationship "spark" with their spouse again.

I've learned that the core to any good relationship is valuing and respecting yourself. When you truly value and respect yourself, you trust yourself. You then will attract people that will respect you.

It took five years and thousands of dollars to become well-trained in life coaching and energy healing. I also have been able to take my personal life lessons and incorporate them into the training I received.

Now I am in a relationship with the man I have waited for all my life. The right man was there all along; I just was hiding behind fear and didn't love myself enough to believe that I deserved real love. It is never too late to live life to its fullest and to speak your truth. It is never too late to love full out and to understand it is your Divine right to live this beautiful life.

Rachel Valliere

Rachel Valliere is a book designer and the founder of Printed Page Studios. She specializes in helping nonfiction authors grow their impact, income, and authority through collaborative, research-driven design. She has been featured in *Forbes* and has designed hundreds of books for a wide variety of authors, including Grant Cardone.

www.printedpagestudios.com

BOOKS SHOULD BE BEAUTIFUL

Rachel Valliere

My first job after graduating college paid eight dollars an hour.

I graduated right after the 2008 financial crisis with a bachelor's in journalism and was spit out into a tough job market in an even tougher town. At the time, newly married, my priority was to find *any* job with health insurance. The best I could do was a position as a bank teller.

I hated the job and felt totally defeated. It wasn't long before I came across a job listing titled "Book Designer." I had never heard of such a thing, but it sounded amazing.

There was plenty of evidence that *book designer* might be the perfect vocation for me. It sounded like a magical compilation of all the things that had brought me joy as a child. I had been an artsy kid, always drawing and writing stories. From a young age, I was an avid reader. I loved going to the library, perusing books, and smelling the pages. At home, I played librarian and made alphabetized tags to affix to my book spines. I was enamored with the printed page. At age ten I wrote and designed a family newsletter. I proudly sold my "independently published" work at our Labor Day cookout for ten cents each—my first career success.

I immediately applied for the book design position and landed it.

By my mid-twenties, I was living the life I thought I had always wanted. I was working as a book designer, my husband and I bought a lovely house in the country, and we had two horses I could watch grazing through the kitchen window. It was a dream come true.

Except . . . I was utterly miserable.

The reality was that my job seemed to have no opportunity for advancement, leaving me feeling unfulfilled, and my marriage was falling apart. Even after years of counseling, we were still struggling.

My husband had accepted a job that kept him out of town most weeknights. I was working full time and taking care of the house, two dogs, and two horses. We eventually decided I would quit my job to reduce stress in our marriage and make it easier for me to handle everything at home.

I had a dream of starting my own business, and this was my chance. It was an unexpected gift.

But two short months later, we started the divorce process. Suddenly I had no income, no home, no purpose, and no direction. Worse yet, I hated myself for failing at my marriage.

I moved to Texas to stay with a friend, taking only the dog I had brought into the marriage and whatever fit in my car. For the first time in my life, I had total freedom, yet I was frozen with indecision. The lack of any restrictions should have been liberating, but it was paralyzing. There was nothing to ground me, no current to follow—it was like floating untethered in space, weightless and terrified.

I spent more time than I care to think about floundering in a haze of self-loathing and confusion, not knowing what I should do, or even what I *wanted* to do. I needed to find my purpose.

What was I meant to do in this world?

How was I going to support myself?

I had been working as a book designer for nearly six years before I quit my job and landed in Texas. I picked up freelance book design gigs to pay the bills, but I viewed that as temporary. The freelance work didn't pay well, and I was tired of struggling.

Furthermore, while I enjoyed book design and loved the idea of it, I had a deep desire to feel like I was making a difference in the world. Back then, book design still felt trivial to me in the grand scheme of life. I didn't feel like making beautiful books had much of an impact on the world.

I continued taking freelance work while trying to figure out what I was "supposed" to be doing. Over time, I applied for dozens of jobs, but even the ones I thought sounded perfect never panned out. I was desperate for some sense of stability and purpose, but my heart's desire still involved entrepreneurship. I think none of the other jobs worked out because, deep down, I didn't want them to.

I finally realized that my fragmented efforts were sabotaging any chance of success, and I made my first big decision—to take what was right in front of me and grow it.

I went all in on book design. After all, the Universe had consistently closed every other door in my face, and by this point it didn't feel coincidental. I could figure out my "true purpose" later. For now, I was convinced I was meant to remain a self-employed book designer to support myself until I figured out my path.

A new type of journey ensued—one of learning that being a freelancer and being a businesswoman are two very different things. As it turned out, stepping into the identity of an entrepreneur is what finally gave me the fulfillment I had wanted all along. It came from taking full ownership, having a broader role in the process, and finding my niche in the industry—working holistically and collaboratively with authors. This new approach changed everything for me. Not only did I fall in love with my work, but I got better at it through developing my unique method.

Ironically, it was only *after* I realized I didn't need a "world-changing" job in order to feel a sense of purpose that I learned how book design *is* world changing.

The moment I came full circle was witnessed by a huge room full of people. I was attending a speaking and sales training. The coach leading the training was teaching us that it's important to sell as if lives depended on it because our work had the potential to literally save lives.

Many of the people in the room were coaches, doctors, healers—helping people recover from pain, grief, and trauma, live lit-up lives, or grow their wealth ... truly life-altering work. I didn't see how book design could ever fit into that category. I wasn't changing lives—just designing books. People can live without that. My old niggles and confusion returned.

I tentatively raised my hand and spoke into the microphone I was handed, explaining how I didn't think this applied to me. The coach asked, "Who are your clients?"

I answered, "Nonfiction authors who are writing a book to grow their business, impact, and audience."

"What's an example of a book you've designed?" he asked.

The project I was currently finishing came to mind. I said, "The most recent one is called *Real Decarbonization*. The author is the CEO of a company she founded that helps oil and gas industry leaders decarbonize."

The coach pressed on. "And what happens if we don't decarbonize?"

I blindly plowed on with my response. Halfway through explaining that decarbonization prevents the literal destruction of the planet that sustains all humanity, I finally saw the light. As the room witnessed the dawning on my face, everyone burst into laughter, including me.

Of all the books to have been working on at that time, it was one about saving the freaking planet. It was a goosebumps moment.

Since then, I haven't questioned the importance of my small role in helping people share their stories. I love what I do, and I know that it's meaningful. Book design not only helps market and sell more books, it also makes the reader's experience more pleasant by adding beauty. Books decorate homes and last lifetimes. They are knowledge encapsulated. Designing beautiful books helps ensure they're read and enjoyed—fulfilling their true purpose.

I believe every type of work is meaningful. Whether it's baking cupcakes or selling car insurance, the energy and intention we bring to our work and the interactions we have with others has a far greater impact than we can ever know.

So what is a book, at its heart, and why does design matter?

A book is a story, a legacy preserved. A story is an account of events, whether fact or fiction. Story is what changes people's minds and opinions—not a list of facts or a debate on social media. Stories help us connect, understand, and find common ground.

Stories change the world. A book is a vehicle for sharing stories. Design is a vehicle for sharing books.

Design is communication—it helps convey a message and gets people to pick up a book and read it. There is nothing trivial about that. Beauty, aesthetics, also bring value—both in the act of creation and the act of consumption.

The entire universe is filled with beautiful things—abstract clouds, vibrant flowers, gnarly trees, breathtaking galaxies. We ourselves are beautiful. I founded Printed Page Studios because books should be beautiful, too.

Today I have the joy and honor of partnering with authors to help them fulfill their life's work—all while having fun designing, nerding out over books, and working from home with my dog snoring softly behind me.

"I have been emboldened now to reduce my experience to the printed page, because I am now less concerned about what 'they say' than I was in the years that have passed."
—*Napoleon Hill,* Think and Grow Rich

CPSIA information can be obtained
at www.ICGtesting.com
Printed in the USA
LVHW021721270523
748196LV00002B/13